Common-Property Arrangements and Scarce Resources

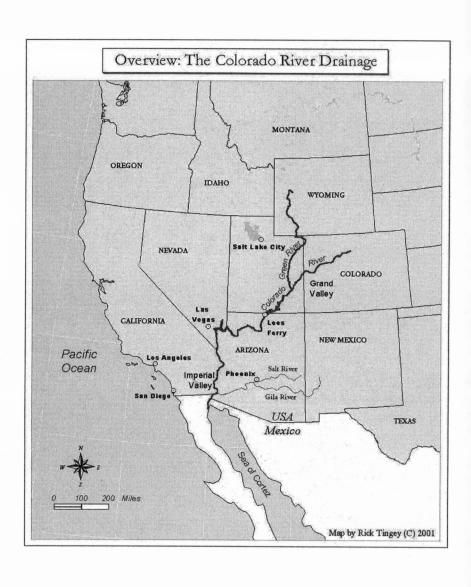

Overview: The Colorado River Drainage

Map by Rick Tingey (C) 2001

Common-Property Arrangements and Scarce Resources

Water in the American West

EDWARD M. BARBANELL

Westport, Connecticut
London

363.61
B22c

Library of Congress Cataloging-in-Publication Data

Barbanell, Edward.
   Common-property arrangements and scarce resources : water in the
American West / Edward M. Barbanell.
      p.   cm.
   Includes bibliographical references and index.
   ISBN 0–275–97173–2 (alk. paper)
   1. Water-supply—West (U.S.)   2. Natural resources, Communal—West
(U.S.)   I. Title.
TD223.6.B37   2001
363.6'1'0978—dc21   2001032908

British Library Cataloguing in Publication Data is available.

Library of Congress Catalog Card Number: 2001032908
ISBN: 0–275–97173–2

First published in 2001

Praeger Publishers, 88 Post Road West, Westport, CT 06881
An imprint of Greenwood Publishing Group, Inc.
www.praeger.com

Printed in the United States of America

∞™

The paper used in this book complies with the
Permanent Paper Standard issued by the National
Information Standards Organization (Z39.48–1984).

10 9 8 7 6 5 4 3 2 1

Angry as one may be at what heedless men have done and still do to a noble habitat, one cannot be pessimistic about the West. This is the native home of hope. When it fully learns that cooperation, not rugged individualism, is the quality that most characterizes and preserves it, then it will have achieved itself and outlived its origins. Then it has a chance to create a society to match its scenery.

Wallace Stegner, *The Sound of Mountain Water*

Contents

Preface

There is a widely held belief among philosophers and economists that all scarce resources are utilized best when their use is controlled through a well-functioning system of private property rights, or private ownership. The aim of this book is to undermine that belief by arguing that for at least one important resource—water in the American West—another form of ownership, what I call a common-property arrangement, is a preferable and achievable alternative to private ownership. In the course of laying out that argument, several conceptual issues arise about the nature of resources, the structure of property rights, and the relationship between the two. By sorting out some of those more general issues, I offer an expanded framework of ownership, or rights-relationships, within which to discuss and attempt to resolve a variety of problems associated with resource scarcity.

The concerns that ignited this project are more than merely academic; they are practical as well as theoretical. The practical concern is simply this, that in much of the American West, water is fast becoming a critically scarce resource. The Colorado River, the major source of water for much of the region, has become so degraded and depleted that the entire pattern of water use there must change quite extensively, and soon. Demonstrating that water in the West is, in fact, critically scarce, a task undertaken in chapter 1, serves to counter recent arguments that no claims about the long-run scarcity of any particular resource need to be taken seriously enough to engender sweeping changes in how that resource is used. The existing pattern of water use in the West cannot be sustained, and the people who live there and rely on that water will be forced into a new relationship with both one another and the river that they all share.

The existing pattern of water use in the American West is a relic from the nineteenth century. It is the enduring manifestation of a view, wholeheartedly embraced by Anglo settlers who began coming to the region in the 1840s, that natural resources should be exploited to their fullest in the name of rapid economic development. To that end, the settlers developed the doctrine of prior appropriation, unique to the American West, which bestowed secure, exclusive, and transferable rights to the first person who was able to put water to some beneficial use. Understanding how that doctrine developed, and why it is no longer justifiable, is the subject of chapter 2. Before the existing pattern of water use in the West can change, the current system of water rights, a system that underlies and serves to perpetuate the existing pattern of use, must itself undergo a substantial transformation. That system of rights, what amounts to a system of private ownership, is no longer conducive to the wise use of a critically scarce resource like water in the West.

Despite the development over the last hundred years or so of a quite fertile conceptual framework for describing and analyzing various sorts of rights-relationships, alternatives to private ownership have been both neglected and misunderstood in the literature. And notwithstanding the fact that the scarcity of water and other natural resources has only recently become a manifest possibility, there has been little conceptual work done on the variable nature of resources. Failure to explore adequately both different forms of ownership and differences between resources has served to render private ownership more attractive than it really is. In chapter 3, I begin an exploration of these more general issues by laying down the conceptual foundations on which to build a normative account of a common-property arrangement for water in the West. After first setting out the central tenets of the dominant framework for discussing property rights and their relationship to one another, I then describe how a common-property arrangement fits within that framework. In the final part of the chapter, I establish three criteria for analyzing differences between resources: jointness, divisibility, and excludability. The extent to which a resource exhibits each of these features constitutes the basis for determining which form of ownership is best suited to it.

Although philosophers have paid little, if any, attention to the particular problems associated with water in the West, this has not dissuaded some economists from claiming that John Locke's seventeenth-century account of how private property rights legitimately emerge from an original state of nature provides the descriptive and normative basis for the western doctrine of prior appropriation. Locke says little about water, but what he does say suggests that he thinks water should be subject to private ownership under the sorts of conditions confronted by western settlers in the nineteenth century. However, as I argue in chapter 4, Locke gives insufficient attention to how resources differ from one another. I maintain, further, that there is room within the structure of Locke's account of property for justifying different rights-relationships for different kinds of resources. In other words, if Locke had inspected the differences between resources in a less-cursory fashion, he may well have objected to the bestowment to individuals of extensive private property rights over some of them, including water. My conclusion is that Locke's account of property does not necessarily support the private ownership of water in the West.

The general neglect that philosophers and economists have displayed toward alternatives to private ownership has led them to associate all forms of common property either with state ownership or, more often and most disparagingly, with some type of open-access regime. In the latter state of affairs, everyone is at liberty to use the resource, but no one has either the claim-right to use the resource or the duty to refrain from using it. It is then typically argued that an open-access regime inevitably leads to the resource's overuse and, ultimately, to the regime's demise. In chapter 5, I argue that by erroneously conflating common property with open-access regime, theorists have uncritically assumed that all common-property arrangements will necessarily be plagued by a particular set of problems, variously called "tragedy of the commons," Prisoner's Dilemma, or free-rider problems. Furthermore, I argue that water use in the West exhibits certain features, that is, certain kinds of negative externality effects, that are not found in the standard examples offered to illustrate such problems. By (1) distinguishing a common-property arrangement from an open-access regime, and (2) showing that water in the West exhibits externality effects significantly different from those typically assumed in discussing Prisoner's Dilemma and the like, I thereby deflate some of the more pernicious arguments against a common-property arrangement for water in the West.

In the final chapter, I describe an alternative to the Prisoner's Dilemma model of human behavior, the Assurance Game. I outline a particular conception of that model, one under which a common-property arrangement might develop and prove successful for combating the degradation and depletion of water in the West. I first argue that such a model provides us with a better account of people's behavior than do various versions of the Prisoner's Dilemma. In the Prisoner's Dilemma, it is assumed that individuals are always motivated only by narrow self-interest, and that no individual will willingly contribute to the common good. In an Assurance Game, given certain conditions, individuals may well prefer to make such contributions. I describe those conditions; I argue that when a group of individuals is able to generate mutual expectations about one another's cooperative behavior, the requisite initiative for enough of them to cooperate and contribute to some common good may be activated and maintained. I then go on to discuss how these conditions might be created in the Colorado River basin, and how, therefore, the basin's inhabitants might move toward establishing a successful common-property arrangement for water in the West.

One final prefatory note is in order. State ownership plays a minor role in this book. In the literature I review, it is more or less assumed that state ownership makes sense only if the marketplace proves totally unworkable. I share that assumption. If one is persuaded that a common-property arrangement is a conceptually sound and practically viable alternative to the private ownership of water in the West, one may nonetheless believe that state ownership is preferable to either. While I do not believe that is the case, I have done little in this book to assay that belief. Thus, a more thorough comparison of common-property arrangements with state ownership represents the basis for an expansion of the analysis offered here.

This book could not have been brought to publication without the help of the following individuals: Peter Diamond, Leslie P. Francis, Don Garrett, Bruce Landesman, James Sabin, Cynthia Stark, and Mildred Vasan. Its timely completion was made possible through the generous financial support provided by the Marriner S. Eccles Foundation and the Steffensen Cannon family. Finally, I would like to thank my wife, Melissa Barbanell, for her patience and understanding. I will always be more grateful to her than I can ever express in words.

Taking Scarcity Seriously

Scarcity is a presumption of all sensible talk about property. If it were ever to fail ... then the traditional problem of the nature and justification of rival types of property systems would probably disappear.

Jeremy Waldron, *The Right to Private Property*

INTRODUCTION

Eventually, in every society, some important resource becomes scarce enough that questions about how and by whom it should be used become central to debates about social justice and public policy. Such is the case in the American West, where water's relative scarcity is the prevailing environmental reality. The following chapters explore several historical, economic, and philosophical issues concerning this state of affairs: how it came about, and what we can and should do now to rectify the situation. The purpose of this chapter, however, is to clarify and defend the putative fact that in the Colorado River basin (see map), water is a critically scarce resource, such that the entire pattern of water use in the region must undergo a substantial transformation.

Most of those who have studied directly the problems associated with water use in the West readily agree that the existing laws, policies, and institutions are incapable of providing enough water to sustain the existing pattern of use.[1] However, there are theorists who insist that no claim about the critical scarcity of a particular resource, and the need to change significantly the social institutions surrounding it, will stand up to careful scrutiny. In particular, the philosopher Jan Narveson argues that those who make such claims often do not understand adequately either the nature of resources or the conditions required to demonstrate their scarcity; he therefore concludes that any claims "that we humans ought to be making great efforts to see to it that our successors . . . will be at least as well provided as we are with this or that are, quite literally, baseless."[2]

Narveson's account commands our attention for two reasons: he offers us a rich conceptual framework within which to assess claims about a resource's critical scarcity, and he gives us compelling reasons for rejecting *most* of those sorts of claims. However, I argue that his failure to consider carefully enough the case of water in the West causes him to overgeneralize his conclusion that *no* claim about the immediate or impending long-run scarcity of a particular resource needs to be taken seriously. Some important resources are scarce enough to warrant significant changes in the way we go about using them, changes that will require a concentrated and concerted effort on the part of those who rely on them, and water in the West is one of those resources.

Narveson's rejection of such scarcity claims relies on certain historical and empirical observations that he thinks are applicable to all of today's important resources. He does not claim that there could *in theory* be no critically scarce resources; rather, he maintains, less sweepingly, that there does not now exist, nor is there likely to exist in the foreseeable future, any resource that will *in fact* meet his proposed test.

However, there are those who maintain that any proposed test for evaluating the critical scarcity of a particular resource is bound to be defective. The political theorist Nicholas Xenos insists that both "scarcity" and its opposite, "abundance," must remain elusive concepts, at least within the confines of the reigning political and economic doctrine; otherwise, industrial capitalism would lose "its raison d'être and its legitimacy."[3] Xenos argues that attempts to adequately characterize "scarcity" routinely suffer from a failure to distinguish *real* needs and desires from *socially created* ones. This constantly changing benchmark serves to relativize "scarcity," thereby undercutting the theoretical ground upon which normative discussions about resource scarcity ultimately rest.[4] Xenos insists that discussions about the scarcity of this or that particular resource reflect nothing more than a particular ideological outlook about certain ways of life and standards of living.

Xenos's critique has little, if any, bearing on the case at hand. At its core, the claim that water is critically scarce in the West amounts to this: There is not enough water for westerners *to continue to live as they do now*, pursuing their same ends in the same ways. As one historian of the West puts it, "In the modern West, the immediate, foreseeable threat . . . is to an established standard of living, to a margin of wastefulness, and to a future of unrestrained economic growth."[5] Narveson's claim is just the opposite: That *nowhere* are current goals or lifestyles threatened in *any* important way by the putative fact that there is not enough of this or that particular resource to go around. Both of these claims use the same benchmark for measuring scarcity, and Xenos's concerns are not at issue here.

Narveson's position is that even if we believe quite strongly that the supply of this or that particular resource is limited or will be exhausted in such and such a period of time, that belief need not worry us very much. He insists that the general historical fact that "our needs and interests are ever changing," combined with our "increasingly efficient utilization of every kind of stuff" leads to the conclusion that there is no "inherent reason to think that we will run out of resources in any reasonably foreseeable future."[6] For any resource we care to consider, an examination of history will show that we will be able either to find more of the stuff, or to find better ways of using it, or to find that we can live without it altogether: That is, either its *availability* will be increased, or its *renewability* will be enhanced, or its *substitutability* will be discovered. Narveson's position is, in essence, that any scarcity problems we are likely to encounter can and probably will be solved by some kind of *technological innovation*, such that people's current ways of life and standards of living will not be threatened in any appreciable way. As John D. McRuer puts it, such a belief reflects an attitude that "human skill can prevail against all, [and that] society can grow forever in wealth and wisdom, and thus in bliss."[7]

While such a "techno-fixer" attitude may be perfectly reasonable for most other important resources, I argue that it is an entirely unreasonable one to take with regard to water in the West.

In this chapter, I briefly describe the current state of water resources in the West. The focus here and throughout this book is on the Colorado River, whose waters are the lifeblood for much of the region. After establishing the fact that there is not presently enough water in the river to sustain the current pattern of water use, I then go on to address in turn Narveson's three other conditions for taking such claims seriously: substitutability, availability, and renewability.

Although it does not take much of an argument to show that water is a *nonsubstitutable* means for achieving many of the ends that will continue to be important to westerners, a more general examination of the concept of a "resource" reveals how water is different from other necessary resources, for example, food and energy.

After addressing substitutability, I go on to discuss availability. I argue that despite our past successes with water and other important resources, and notwithstanding our considerable technological know-how, there is little likelihood that more water will in fact be made available to westerners; they will simply have to learn to make do with existing supplies.

Finally, I address the question of renewability. While it is true that water is, potentially, a perfectly renewable resource, I argue that the intensive use of water in the West has degraded and depleted the resource to such a degree that it no longer *is* renewing itself. The conclusion is that, all things considered, Narveson's general complacency about running out of this or that resource is not warranted in the case of water in the West.

A RIVER NO MORE

The Colorado River is the primary source of surface water for a large portion of the American West. In all, a 244,000–square-mile region comprised of cities, suburbs, farms, and untamed wilderness spread out over a seven-state area about the size of modern-day France. "The river system provides over half the water of greater Los Angeles, San Diego, and Phoenix; it grows much of America's domestic production of fresh winter vegetables; it illuminates the neon city of Las Vegas."[8] Although there is a vast quantity of water stored in underground aquifers, so-called groundwater, its limited renewability and diminishing availability precludes it from being a long-term solution to the West's water ills; further discussion of groundwater is discussed later in this chapter, where availability and renewability are, in turn, examined in some detail. Here, the focus is on the river system and how its water is currently put to use.

The substance of the claim that water is critically scarce in the West amounts to this: The supply of Colorado River water is limited, and we have reached if not exceeded that limit. Actually, there are two, interconnected limits at issue here, one having to do with the *quantity* of water, the other with its *quality*. The claim is that *both* of these limits have been reached: There is not enough water available, and what is available is of such a diminished quality that westerners must now be very careful about how they go about using it. Issues about water quality fall under the more general problem of water pollution. Narveson's contention is that pollution, and in particular water pollution, is not a serious problem. He maintains that polluted water can always be cleaned up: "with a certain amount of reprocessing ... it's ready to go around again."[9] Questions about the quality of Colorado River water, then, are closely connected to issues about its renewability, which are discussed later on. Here, I am primarily concerned with the limited quantity of the river's water available for the variety of uses to which it is presently put. Some of these uses require water of a particular quality, and the claim is that the available quantity of water *of this quality* is no longer sufficient to support all these uses at their current levels. Already, in places like Los Angeles and San Diego, "the water is so salty that restaurants often serve it with a slice of lemon. If you pour it on certain plants, they will die."[10]

Over most of its 1,450–mile journey to its destination, the Gulf of California (or the Sea of Cortez), the Colorado River travels through a region naturally ill-suited to human habitation. Other than at its source high in the Rocky Mountains, the river runs through territory that receives, on average, less than ten inches of rainfall annually. Such territory will not support farming that depends on water falling from the sky.[11] In order to grow their crops, farmers must irrigate their fields with water diverted out of the river. Agriculture currently accounts for 80 percent to 90 percent of the region's water use; most of the water used for irrigation is rendered unavailable for further use: it either evaporates, is transpired by the crops, or is absorbed into the soil.[12] The water that does eventually return to the river is many times saltier than when it was diverted out of the river, which causes a variety of problems downstream. The fact that over most of its length the river courses through deep canyons and inhospitable deserts means that the region's population centers are often located far away from their primary source of water; city dwellers must also divert water not only to sate their thirst, but also to keep their lawns green and their pools filled. Because of all the damming, storing, diverting, and using going on, the Colorado River no longer reaches its destination, and has not for almost forty years. Just a few miles south of the Morelos Dam on the U.S.-Mexico border, the last of the Colorado River vanishes into the sands of the Baja Desert, its meager trickle too salty to grow crops, too scant to support wildlife, and too poisonous to bathe in or drink. It is, as Philip L. Fradkin puts it, "a river no more."[13]

On average, there are about fourteen million acre-feet of Colorado River water available every year. Once you subtract the two million acre-feet that evaporates annually from Lake Mead, Lake Powell, and the region's other man-made reservoirs, the figure is actually closer to twelve million. An acre-foot represents the volume of water it would take to cover one acre of land with one foot of water, or about 326,000 gallons; the typical western family of five uses about one acre-foot of water per year for personal consumption.[14] Today, every acre-foot of Colorado River water is either already being used or otherwise spoken for. The river's waters were divided up among the seven states it flows through in the historic Colorado River Compact of 1922, the only interstate agreement of its kind that the federal government has ever ratified.[15] Using a figure of 16.5 million acre-feet, a figure derived from measuring the river's flow over what we now realize were uncharacteristically wet years, the states (reluctantly) set aside 1.5 million acre-feet for Mexico and split the rest equally between the upper-basin states (Colorado, New Mexico, Wyoming, and Utah) and the lower-basin states (Arizona, California, and Nevada). In 1948, the four upper-basin states agreed how to apportion their combined 7.5 million acre-feet among themselves; and after years of legal battles, the lower-basin states followed suit. In the beginning of 1997, actual water use in the entire basin stood at just under twelve million acre-feet, or just about at the replenishment rate. In the summer of that year, Arizona completed a diversion project that allowed it to use its entire allotment of 2.8 million acre-feet, pushing the basin's total use above the 13 million mark.[16] In other words, the river is now operating at a deficit, and it cannot sustain the current level of diversions for long.

Despite the fact that the basin's states cannot collectively utilize their entire agreed-upon allotment, some states at present use more than they are legally entitled to. For example, southern California's annual allotment of Colorado River water under the Colorado River Compact is 4.5 million acre-feet, yet its actual yearly use now exceeds 5 million acre-feet. The main culprit, the Metropolitan Water District (MWD) of southern California, has been warned by both the federal government and neighboring states that it must come up with a plan to live within its allotment. Water-starved San Diego, which currently buys most of its water from the MWD, has been trying to strike a deal with farmers in the nearby Imperial Irrigation District (IID) to buy their "excess" water. The MWD is suing to stop the deal; it argues that since the IID's water would be flowing through the MWD's aqueducts on its way to San Diego, the MWD should be able to collect whatever use-fees it sees fit. The Coachella Irrigation District, next to the IID, has also threatened to sue to stop the deal, arguing that it should receive for free any "saved" water that IID does not use. Its claim is based on the western doctrine of prior appropriation, discussed in chapter 2, under which excess or saved water is available for capture and use by anyone else.[17] The Colorado River is well living up to its reputation as "the most legislated, most debated, and most litigated river in the entire world."[18]

It seems quite clear that under existing laws, policies, and patterns of use, there is no longer enough water available in the region; for those who rely on water from the Colorado River, there is simply no more river. Because of the depleted and degraded state of the resource, westerners cannot continue to operate as they have, using the river's water in the ways and at the levels currently exhibited. And for reasons adduced in the rest of this chapter, this state of affairs constitutes water's critical scarcity in the West.

SUBSTITUTABILITY

Narveson characterizes a "resource" broadly and simply as anything that people can or do use as a means to an end. Since both our ends and the ways we go about trying to achieve them are continually changing, the importance of any particular resource is itself subject to change. "To the cavemen, aluminum was not a resource, while smooth, flattish, elongated stones probably were. For the modern car manufacturer, and most modern consumers, it's decidedly the other way around."[19] In other words, the importance of a resource can be measured along a sliding scale. At one end of the scale are those resources needed for our very survival; at the other end are luxury items, those used to satisfy people's less-pressing desires. As both our abilities (i.e., technology) and desires change, the position of a resource along this scale varies. Some resources may fall off the scale altogether, whereas others may suddenly command our attention for the very first time.

Narveson maintains that in order to take seriously claims about a resource's scarcity, it must be shown not only that the stuff in question is a necessary, or nonsubstitutable, means for achieving a particular end, but also that the end itself will continue to be important to us. He readily admits that water is, and will continue to be, an irreplaceable means for at least one end that will continue to be important to us—namely, survival.[20] However, one sort of argument that Narveson does find problematic, and rightly so, is when the resource in question is something no less necessary than water but much less specific than it, such as food or energy. The problem here is that the resource in question is often conceived of too broadly. Take, for instance, the economist Timothy D. Tregarthen's position: "Water's essentiality hardly makes it unique. Life would also be awkward without food, clothing, and shelter, none of which present particular problems."[21] But to substitute food for water in an argument about necessary means to important ends renders the argument much less persuasive, for one could reasonably counter that there are all sorts of foodstuffs available. Though we do need food, there is no *particular* foodstuff upon which our survival depends. If, for instance, wheat was in limited supply, or we had a reasonable belief that our supplies of wheat would be exhausted in a short period of time, we could substitute it with corn or some other grain. Life might well be awkward without wheat, but without water it would be well nigh impossible, and therein lies the difference.[22]

Similarly, just as there are many specific kinds of food, there are as well any of a multitude of means available for generating energy. If someone were to argue that we *need* oil, it could be countered that we survived quite well, thank you, long before the invention of the internal combustion engine. And more importantly, regardless of whatever purposes we have found for using oil, adequate substitutes have been and continue to be developed: coal, natural gas, solar power, wind, and even water.

With regard to things like food and energy then, both their broad character and the substitutability of any specific manifestation of them makes claims about their critical scarcity much less compelling than those about water's.[23]

So, water is a resource that is essential for ends that, for the foreseeable future, will continue to be important; no other resource can be substituted for it. However, water is used in both *direct* and *indirect* ways: not only do westerners use water for drinking and other domestic purposes, but they also use it to mine for precious metals, to drive hydroelectric turbines, and to produce a variety of agricultural products. The distinction between a direct and an indirect use of a particular resource can be characterized, roughly, by saying that where it is only a raw material or other component used in a process designed to produce some other, final good, then the resource is used indirectly; where the resource *is* the final good, then we use the resource directly. Few resources are either always or only used directly or indirectly, and water in the West is clearly used as both a raw (indirect) and a final (direct) good. The distinction between direct and indirect uses is helpful in assessing Narveson's contention that "resource scarcity is predicated on continued interest in the purposes served by the stuffs in question, but there is little certainty that we will continue to have the specific interests served only by the stuff in point."[24]

Westerners will, with much certainty, have a continued interest in a final good such as energy, but the production of energy does not *require* water as a raw material: there are many other means or resources available for generating it (coal, solar power, and so on). And in the West, mining with water is no longer of much concern. The first major influx of Anglo settlers in the West, in the 1840s, was precipitated by the discovery of gold in California, and the miners required large quantities of water in order to work their mining claims.[25] While it may well have been the case that in the 1840s there were no other means available for mining, the enterprise of surface mining has been largely abandoned and is no longer a central issue in discussions about western water use.

Such facts seem to suggest, and some might argue, that it is only westerners' direct need for water with which we should be concerned, because their other specific though indirect interests can be adequately served by other raw materials. That is, even where certain ends for which water is now a means will probably continue to be important, there is little certainty that water will continue to be a means to those ends. So, the argument might go, if water's scarcity for direct, nonsubstitutable use in the West is a result of its indirect, substitutable uses for other purposes, then its scarcity for direct use can be overcome by simply making the required substitutions for its indirect uses.

There are, however, several problems with such an argument, only one of which I will discuss here. First and foremost, agriculture is one indirect use of water that has been and continues to be something in which westerners have a significant interest. More than 80 percent of all the water used in the West is withdrawn from its source and used for irrigating crops; in Arizona, that figure approaches 90 percent. We of course do need food, and we need water in order to produce it, but the obvious rejoinder, one made by both techno-fixers and deep ecologists alike, is that although we must grow crops, it is far from necessary to practice large-scale agriculture in the arid West. Crops in any kind of quantity can only be grown there by irrigating them—an expensive and wasteful process that, because of the ecological harm it has wrought, cannot reasonably be expected to continue to be practiced much longer. Moreover, more than a third of all irrigated acres in the West are used to grow alfalfa and other crops that are grown to feed cows. Not only do such crops require much more water per acre than do most crops consumed directly by human beings, but also one cow requires as many calories as it takes to sustain five to ten people.[26]

But insofar as moving away from large-scale agriculture, or altering what is grown or how it is grown, is a necessary response to water's scarcity in the region, such changes will require major shifts in the entire social and economic order of the region. People's livelihoods and ways of life will have to be recast in relatively dramatic fashion. Yet as I have already indicated, explicit in Narveson's discussion of resource scarcity is the attitude that nothing is so scarce as to require much of a change in how we live our lives, and that instituting the required substitution of means and/or ends will be a rather prosaic and not-too-painful process. But this is simply not true in the American West.

AVAILABILITY

In order to take seriously the claim that a particular resource is critically scarce, Narveson contends that in addition to identifying it as a necessary means to an end that will continue to be important in the foreseeable future, our estimate of how much of it is available is not likely to be revised. And history, he contends, has so far borne out the fallacy of such claims: We have been able to make more arable land available by reclaiming it from the ocean or by transforming inhospitable deserts into thriving oases; and we have increased crop yields though myriad technological innovations. Time and again, in all cases of the predicted scarcity of things we thought we could not do without, we have either been able to find more of the stuff, or, where this has failed, we have been able to make more of the stuff we have found available for use. For instance, the prediction that we would run out of oil in thirty or so years, a popular belief in the 1960s, was predicated on how much oil could be extracted under low pressure. This amount, however, "is perhaps a tenth of what one can get by pumping it under high pressure," as is now the norm.[27] More generally, this example points to the fact that what "exists" is often more extensive than what is currently "available": The claim that no more of a particular resource is currently available is not the same thing as claiming that no more of it exists. If there is arable land on Mars, then there exists more arable land than is currently available.

As a matter of the West's history, we have in fact demonstrated an ability both to find more water and to make use of water sources that were known to exist but heretofore considered unavailable. Through advances in hydrology, vast reserves of groundwater were discovered under the West's deserts. Hydrologists have estimated that, prior to its intensive use and depletion, there was thirty-seven times more water underground than there was on the surface; and the invention of the centrifugal pump, shortly after World War I, made this ground-water available for use.[28] In addition, technological advances have allowed westerners to move vast amounts of water from where it was to where it was needed; for example, in the early years of this century the Owens River in California was completely diverted from its natural course and made to flow to Los Angeles, over 250 miles away.[29]

Such examples would seem to concede the very point at issue, namely, that current estimates of how much water is currently available in the West are an unreliable guide for predicting how much of it either exists or can be made available in the future. Since westerners have a good track record of finding more water and making more of it available for use, to maintain that the region's supply of water is, practically speaking, either physically limited or will be exhausted in so many years has no prima facie support.

History, however, is a poor guide here. All things considered, there are indeed good reasons for believing that, for the foreseeable future, no more water will be made available to westerners. While it is true that we are not running out of water in any absolute sense, we are running out of supplies of it that can be utilized within the ambit of economics, technology, and, perhaps most importantly, our ever-growing concern for the quality of our environment.

Of known terrestrial sources,[30] the vast reserves of water lying beneath the western deserts have sometimes been touted as the region's salvation. There are, however, two interconnected reasons for believing that the West's redemption will not come from underground water, or "groundwater": For all practical purposes it is nonrenewable, and at the current rate of withdrawal it will likely be gone in fifty to one hundred years.[31] It is not just a matter of technology and economics; inventing better water pumps will not get around the simple fact that we are using up the groundwater much faster than it can be replenished. It is not only environmentalists who make such claims, but also western state officials who have in the past actively promoted the "mining" of groundwater. The state water engineer of New Mexico for much of the 1980s, Stephen Reynolds, admits "We made a conscious decision to mine out our share of [the groundwater] in a period of twenty-five to forty years."[32] In short, mining groundwater will not even partially satisfy the West's current desire for more water. If more water is to be made available it must come from other known sources.

If the total amount of fresh surface water is considered, then it seems clear that plenty of it exists, not only for use in the West, but also for anyone who needs it—again, no one claims that we are running out of water in any absolute sense. For technological and economic reasons—not to mention political ones—the idea that untapped water supplies in Asia, for example, will be transported to Utah to irrigate alfalfa fields is not seriously entertained. Yet one need not look far outside the American West to find vast and unused supplies of fresh water. When Reynolds and his counterparts in other western states were asked what they would do when their groundwater was depleted, they said "when we use it up, we'll just have to get more water from somewhere else."[33] The somewhere else they had in mind was the Canadian province of British Columbia, where there are, either in whole or in part, the third-, fourth-, seventh-, eighth-, and nineteenth-largest rivers in North America (the Colorado River does not even rank in the top twenty-five). It is debatable how much of the *world's* accessible and renewable fresh water the province holds, but the usual estimates are between 4 percent and 10 percent.[34] Just as the water of the Owens and other western rivers has in the past been diverted to where it was needed, the most common refrain from techno-fixers is that in the future we can simply divert these other rivers–including those as far away as the Yukon River in Alaska–to sate the thirst of an ever-growing desert population.

There are no insurmountable technological impediments to making such water available to westerners. In fact, in the 1950s and 1960s, a proposal called the North American Water and Power Alliance (NAWAPA) was developed and promoted to do just that. Here is one commentator's description of what NAWAPA would look like:

Visualize a series of towering dams in the deep river canyons of British Columbia—dams 800, 1,500, even 1,700 feet high. Visualize reservoirs backing up behind them for hundreds of miles—reservoirs among which Lake Mead would be merely regulation size. Visualize the flow of the Susitna River, the Copper, the Tanana, and the upper Yukon running in reverse, pushed through the Saint Elias Mountains by million-horsepower pumps, then dumped into nature's second largest reservoir, the Rocky Mountain Trench. . . . [T]he trench would serve as the continent's hydrologic switching yard, storing 400 million acre-feet of water in a reservoir 500 miles long. The upper Columbia and Fraiser [Rivers], which flow in opposite directions in the Rocky Mountain Trench, would disappear under it. . . . [Visualize] a battery of airplane-hangar siphons shooting 30,000 cubic feet of water per second through tunnels in the Sawtooth Range of Idaho and on to California, Nevada, Arizona, and Mexico.[35]

The enormous costs of such a project—estimated at 200 billion dollars in 1964—make it highly unlikely that it will be built in the foreseeable future. But even if the situation changed so drastically that NAWAPA actually made economic sense, the environmental effects would be devastating:

In the Western United States, the plan would drown or dry up just about any section of wild river still left, causing the extirpation of 90 percent of the salmon runs. . . . In Canada and the U.S. alike, not just rivers but an astounding amount of wilderness and wildlife habitat would be put under water, tens of millions of acres of it. Surface aqueducts and siphons would cut off migratory routes. Hundreds of thousands of people would have to be relocated; Prince George, B.C., population 150,000, would vanish from the face of the earth.[36]

And these are just some of the effects that we know about. Yet if we have learned anything from our previous attempts at manipulating nature, it is that the overall effects of our technological acts cannot be foreseen with any kind of certainty. What effects such a permanent relocation of vast amounts of surface water would have on weather patterns alone is a complete mystery. As one hydrologist put it, "the environmental damage that would be caused by [NAWAPA] can't even be described."[37]

Even those economists who are the most vocal advocates of market solutions to the West's water problems admit that we have entered an age of limits, where we have become and should continue to be "doubtful about gigantic projects, about miracles of engineering as solutions to economic problems."[38] And politicians have by and large reached the same conclusion. One reason rivers in Canada and Alaska have been eyed thirstily by westerners is that water sources closer to the region—the Columbia and Snake Rivers, and the Great

Lakes—have been deemed off-limits to them. In fact, federal laws have been enacted that forbid even the allocation of funds to study diversions from these more accessible sources of fresh water.[39] There have even been efforts of late to reverse the whole process, to begin to undo our mutation of the West's landscape. In the late 1980s, the city of Los Angeles returned some water to the Owens River, allowing it to flow in its natural course for the first time in almost half a century. More recently, there have been serious discussions about draining Lake Powell in southern Utah, and resurrecting that labyrinth of red-rocked canyons that now lie entombed beneath its stagnant waters. All of this strongly suggests, and in no uncertain terms, that for the foreseeable future, diverting large amounts of surface water to the Colorado River basin is not a viable option.

What other existing water might be made available to westerners? Of all the water that the earth has today, which is about all the planet will ever have, more than 97 percent of it resides in the oceans and seas as salt water; most of the remaining 3 percent is imprisoned in glaciers and ice caps. (The renewable freshwater supply in the planet's rivers, lakes, and underground aquifers has been estimated to represent a microscopic eight-thousandths of all the water on Earth. Much of the water not in the seas, ice caps, and glaciers is in swamps, or is floating as clouds or invisible vapor in the atmosphere, or is locked up in soils and plant tissues.[40]) The desalinization of sea water is not currently economically feasible: it takes three kilowatt-hours of energy to make just one gallon of fresh water. Even if the process can be made economically feasible, the toxic salt brines that are an inevitable by-product would create a pollution problem of very large dimensions. And although a few individuals have suggested dragging icebergs down from the Arctic Sea, even the most favorable estimates relegate them to a minor, local role.[41]

In short, the facts indicate that, although more water exists than is currently available to westerners, very little if any of it can be expected to be made available to them. Leaving environmental and economic issues to one side, technological advances might *someday* change the facts, but that someday is neither tomorrow nor, by most lights, even twenty-five years from now. And as was discussed earlier, westerners simply cannot wait that long.

RENEWABILITY

The last factor to be considered for taking seriously claims about water's critical scarcity in the West is its renewability. Narveson says that in all claims about a resource's scarcity:

It is assumed that the resources in question are nonrenewable. But in fact food, water, and air are all completely and naturally recycled: all of these resources go in one end of us and come out the other; with a certain amount of reprocessing, at the hands of either nature (always) or man (sometimes), it's ready to go around again. Claims about "shortages," therefore, can only be claims about the length of the renewal cycle. . . . In the case of water, [renewal] takes a little longer and resupply from rain is uneven and not always reliable. But so far as ultimate supply is concerned, it is essentially constant and talk of shortages has only to do with the cost of transportation and purification.[42]

With regard to groundwater, Narveson is clearly mistaken: the water being pumped out of the ground is as nonrenewable as oil. Pumping groundwater reduces the remaining "pile" of it, and just like oil, the replenishment of groundwater occurs in terms of geologic rather than biologic time. While it is true that the groundwater taken out of the aquifers lying beneath the western deserts does re-enter the global water cycle, it falls as rain somewhere else, and we have already discussed the problems with trying to move massive amounts of water from where it is to where it is not.

Leaving groundwater to one side then, we need to assess Narveson's position with regard to the renewability of surface water in the West. Agriculture accounts for the vast majority of Colorado River water used in the region. Not only does irrigation consume this water in a relatively straightforward fashion, intensive irrigation also transforms the water in a more insidious way, mainly by increasing its salinity to levels that, if left unchecked, renders the water unavailable for further use. Such effects are not just foreseeable consequences to be avoided in the future; rather, they are a palpable reality today. The overall effect of such a transformation is that the supply of surface water, rather than being renewed, is being inexorably degraded: using Colorado River water as westerners currently do essentially renders it nonrenewable. And even if westerners can modify how they use this water in order to allow it to renew itself, such changes will require more than merely superficial alterations to the region's social and economic fabric.

Moving downstream from the river's source high in the Rocky Mountains, the Grand Valley in western Colorado is the first of many places along the river's course where there are large-scale diversions of water for irrigation. As is typical in the region, three-quarters of the diverted water either evaporates or is transpired by the crops.

Evaporation can be reduced by, among other things, simply covering irrigation canals. Also, since different crops transpire water at different rates, changing what crops are grown can significantly reduce the amount of water lost. For instance, alfalfa transpires about 85 percent of the water applied to it, whereas orange trees only transpire about 50 percent.[43] So, by upgrading diversion ditches and switching to less water-intensive crops, the amount of water lost through evaporation and transpiration in places like the Grand Valley could be greatly reduced by simply employing available know-how and technology.[44] But even if such changes were implemented, the main, though less-obvious, problem would still exist. The remaining water, whether it is one-quarter or one-half of the originally diverted amount, contains virtually all of the salts that were in the diverted water. In the West, "Salinity is the monkey on irrigation's back. The good water goes up in the sky and the junk water goes down."[45] The problem actually has two aspects: The increased salt content degrades not only the river water but also the soil to which it is applied. And as will become clear, viable solutions to the problem will require different agricultural practices altogether, rather than simply applying technological fixes to existing ones.

Ignoring the fact that irrigated runoff is often contaminated with fertilizer and pesticide residue, the water that remains after evaporation and transpiration has taken its toll is now two to four times saltier than when it was taken out of the river. In many locations, not all of the remaining water will return to the river: some of it is absorbed by the soil; some of it percolates down to underground aquifers; and some of it travels underground, to return to the surface in a different river drainage system. But in places like the Grand Valley, most of the remaining water does return to its source. In doing so, the already salt-laden water must travel through sedimentary salt formations, a ubiquitous feature throughout the Colorado River basin. By the time the water reaches the river again, its salinity level is, on average, thirty-seven times higher than at the diversion point. As it moves downstream, the same water is diverted again and again on its way to the sea; on the Colorado River, the same water may be used eighteen times over.[46] The cumulative effect of this constant reuse is that the river itself becomes saltier and saltier as one moves downstream. At each diversion point, the diverted water is saltier to begin with than it was at upstream diversion points, and the water returning to the river after each application to crops is saltier still. At Lee's Ferry in northern Arizona, the dividing point between the upper and lower river basin, the salt content of the river was about 600 parts per million (ppm) in 1970. Just before crossing the border into Mexico, the salt content of the river in that same year exceeded 2,000 ppm. Such levels spell death for most crops.[47]

Looking at the river's salinity synchronically at different points along its course does not tell the whole story however. Looked at diachronically and at the same point, the salinity of the river is increasing as well. The 600 ppm measured at Lee's Ferry in 1970 was 20 percent higher than the 500 ppm measured in 1940. The best estimates are that by 2010, if the current rate of water use for irrigation continues unaltered, the measured salinity at Lee's Ferry will exceed 800 ppm.[48] So, it is not just that as one moves downstream the water gets saltier; at each point along the river where water is diverted, the river is getting saltier, which only serves to exacerbate the salinity problem downstream.

Another reason why the river's salinity is increasing is that as water evaporates and transpires, some of the salt stays in the soil. That is, the salinity of the soil is increasing over time as well. So not only does the water returning to the river have to pass through sedimentary salt formations, it must first pass through soil that is itself becoming saltier over time. And this buildup of salt in the soil is the second aspect of the salinity problem. As salts build up in the soil and in the root zones of the crops, the plants are not able to absorb water as efficiently as before. In order for farmers to keep growing the same amount of the same crop from year to year, they have to continually increase the amount of water they use. The amount of water needed to mature crops is called the "duty" of water, and it is expressed in terms of the number of acres that a second-foot of water (one cubic foot per second) flowing continuously through the growing season can irrigate. The higher the duty, the better. The buildup of salts in the root zones of crops means that the duty of water decreases because more water is needed for each acre each year. And as more water is applied to the crops, more salt builds up in the soil. The effects of this continual buildup of salt are already being felt: hundreds of thousands of acres of farmland in the West have had to be abandoned due to salinity problems. Once fertile fields, now covered with a crusty salt residue, lay fallow, shimmering like crystal in the noonday sun.[49]

Salinity, of course, is not the only problem engendered by current agricultural practices; it is simply the most damaging and the hardest to rectify. Fertilizer and pesticide residue is also a problem, as is contamination from mine tailings left from an earlier era: water making its way back to the Colorado River often leeches through exposed radioactive and toxic material. Most of the agricultural diversions of water occur upstream from the basin's large population centers: Phoenix, Las Vegas, Los Angeles, and San Diego. Besides making the water taste bad, other tangible effects of such a saline flow are the corrosion of metal pipes and increases in soap consumption and water-softening additives, all of which sharply increase the costs to urban water users.[50] As the salinity of the Colorado River increases, such effects will only get worse.

In short, it seems clear that rather than being renewed, surface water in the Colorado River basin is being insidiously and inexorably degraded. The sense of renewability espoused by Narveson connotes returning a resource to the same overall state it was in prior to its use by human beings. This state is to be assessed not only in terms of its quantity, but also in terms of its quality. With regard to the renewability of water, Narveson maintains that "talk of shortages has only to do with the cost of transportation and purification."[51] Having already discussed the problems associated with transporting large quantities of water, the question remains as to what it would take to renew or even just stabilize the quality of the West's surface water.

Clearly, if we simply stopped diverting water to irrigate crops, or at least greatly reduced such diversions, the degradation of the Colorado River would be greatly retarded.[52] But insofar as curtailing large-scale agriculture in the West is an option, it will require thoroughgoing changes in the entire social order of the region. A less-drastic response is to very carefully manage what crops are actually grown. Some crops are much more tolerant of salt than are others; for example, experimental plots of cotton have been grown with water that has a salt content of 5,900 ppm. The general idea is that crops less tolerant of salt could be grown upstream from crops that are more tolerant of it. Such a response is right in line with techno-fixers' attitude that we have found and will continue to develop better and more efficient ways to use a resource like water, and that we should, therefore, be more sanguine and less apocalyptic about water's putative scarcity in the West. However, such a response would only extend the life of large-scale agriculture in the region, rather than allowing it to continue in perpetuity. It would do nothing to curtail the degradation of either the soil or the water. In addition, it would require individual irrigators to consider their actions in terms of the overall effects to the region. Many of the problems are not felt by those doing the irrigation, but by someone else downstream. In other words, many of the costs of increased salinity represent negative externalities. As will be discussed in chapter 5, the problem of internalizing these externalities is a hindrance to free-market solutions to the region's water ills.

To continue practicing agriculture as it is done now while at the same time renewing the river's water and preventing soil degradation, there are really only two possible solutions, neither of which is very practical. One would be to construct numerous, massive desalinization facilities. Not only are the costs of large-scale desalinization currently prohibitive, but also the resultant toxic salt brines would have to be transported and dumped somewhere else. In the same vein, the other possible solution would be to construct enormous drainage systems underneath irrigated acreage in order to transport the salt-laden water away. But again, this would only serve to flush the problem down to someone else.[53] The salt-laden water could be diluted with fresh water or, alternatively, used in sufficiently large quantities in order to maintain a proper salt balance and prevent crop and soil damage, but where would westerners get the needed quantities of water? Even if such solutions, either alone or in concert, were technologically, economically, and environmentally feasible, there would have to be massive changes to the region's political and social institutions. And it is this fact, more than anything else, that belies the sanguinity implicit in Narveson's and other techno-fixers' attitude about the renewability of surface water in the Colorado River basin.

Enough has been said, I hope, to make it clear that the scarcity of water in large portions of the American West is a problem to be taken quite seriously. The thesis that westerners should work to conserve and sustain their available water supplies should not be open to serious debate. As Richard D. Lamm, the former governor of Colorado, wrote almost twenty years ago, "We cannot produce our way out of our water crises. . . . What we should have learned by now is that we must work on the demand side."[54] Little if any of what has been said about the facts surrounding water use in the West has not already been espoused in great detail in any number of studies published over the last two decades. But these studies, mostly historical in nature, are noticeably silent, vague, or both about what ought to be done going forward: They tell us how and why westerners have gotten themselves into their current predicament, but they shed little light on the future.

The overarching question that animates the rest of this book is what should we do about it? More specifically, the question is: What sorts of property rights would offer the best guarantee that water resources in the West will not continue to be depleted and degraded, and to whom should these rights be given? As the overall character and distribution of property rights serves to define the form of ownership in a particular situation, what is really being asked is: What form of ownership is best suited to a resource water in the West? In the next chapter I begin to address this question by analyzing the current form of ownership for western water and describing how it came about.

NOTES

1. See Terry L. Anderson, "Introduction: The Water Crisis and the New Resource Economics," in *Water Rights: Scarce Resource Allocation, Bureaucracy, and the Environment*, ed. Terry L. Anderson (Cambridge, MA: Ballinger Publishing for the Pacific Institution for Public Policy Research, 1983), 2–5; and William Ophuls, *Ecology and the Politics of Scarcity Revisited* (New York: Freeman, 1992), 9–11.

2. Jan Narveson, "The Concept of Resources and Claims about Global Scarcities," paper presented at the annual meeting of the Canadian Philosophical Association, Memorial University, St. John's, Newfoundland, June 1, 1997; see also Jan Narveson, "Resources and Environmental Policy," *Philosophic Exchange* 23/24 (1993–1994): 39–61.

3. Nicholas Xenos, "Liberalism and the Politics of Scarcity," *Political Theory* 15 (1987): 239.

4. Ibid., 225–243. Xenos gives a more thorough treatment of this topic in *Scarcity and Modernity* (New York: Routledge, 1989). See also Ralph Sassower, "Scarcity and Setting the Boundaries of Political Economy," *Social Epistemology* 4 (1990): 75–91; and Ernest Raiklin and Bulent Uyarm, "On the Relativity of the Concepts of Needs, Wants, Scarcity, and Opportunity Cost," *International Journal of Social Economics* 23, no. 7 (July 1996): 49–57.

5. Donald Worster, *Rivers of Empire: Water, Aridity, and the Growth of the American West* (New York: Random House, Pantheon Books, 1985; reprint, New York: Oxford University Press, 1992), 312.

6. Narveson, "Concept of Resources," 7.

7. John D. McRuer, "Conventions vs. Greens," *World* 63 (March–April 1990): 5–6; see also A. Stephan Boyan Jr., Forward to *Ecology and the Politics of Scarcity*, by William Ophuls (New York: Freeman, 1992), xv–xix.

8. Mark Reisner, *Cadillac Desert: The American West and Its Disappearing Water* (New York: Penguin, 1993), 120.

9. Narveson, "Concept of Resources," 9.

10. Reisner, *Cadillac Desert*, 7.

11. Ibid., 3.

12. See Worster, *Rivers of Empire*, 112, 311; and Reisner, *Cadillac Desert*, 9.

13. Philip L. Fradkin, *A River No More: The Colorado River and the West* (Tucson: University of Arizona Press, 1981); see also Brian Alexander, "Between Two West Coast Cities, a Duel to the Last Drop," *New York Times*, 8 December 1998, 15; Jim Carrier, Introduction to *The Colorado: A River at Risk* (Englewood, CO: Westcliffe, 1992), 18; and Worster, *Rivers of Empire*, 272.

14. Westerners use a profligate amount of water for personal consumption. Whereas the national average for direct personal use is around 90 gallons per day, in Tucson it is 140 gallons; in Denver it is 230. See Worster, *Rivers of Empire*, 312.

15. The best discussion of the Colorado River Compact can be found in Norris Hundley Jr., *Water and the West: The Colorado River Compact and the Politics of Water in the American West* (Berkeley: University of California Press, 1975).

16. The completion of the Central Arizona Project was announced with considerable fanfare. See Dennis Cauchon, "Arizona Takes Its Full Share of River," *USA Today*, 17 October 1997, 3.

17. See Alexander, "Between Two West Coast Cities," 1; and Todd S. Purdum, "U.S. Acts to Meet Water Needs in the West," *New York Times*, 19 December 1997, A9.

18. Reisner, *Cadillac Desert*, 120.

19. Narveson, "Concept of Resources," 4.

20. Narveson, "Resources and Environmental Policy," 41.

21. Timothy D. Tregarthen, "Water in Colorado: Fear and Loathing of the Marketplace," in *Water Rights*, ed. Terry L. Anderson (Cambridge, MA: Ballinger Publishing for the Pacific Institute for Public Policy Research, 1983), 120.

22. See Stephen P. Munzer, *A Theory of Property* (Cambridge: Cambridge University Press, 1990), 274–276.

23. When the end for which a particular resource is needed can reasonably be expected to be of only temporary or passing interest, claims about its continuing importance are even less compelling. And a good case can be made that, as an empirical matter, many ends and the means for achieving them have proved ephemeral. The scarcity of intercontinental ballistic missiles seemed of paramount importance for roughly forty years; today, we worry about the scarcity of effective means for destroying them.

24. Narveson, "Concept of Resources," 8.

25. See chapter 2; and Donald J. Pisani, *Water, Land, and Law in the West* (Lawrence: University of Kansas Press, 1996), 11–13, 24–37.

26. See Reisner, *Cadillac Desert*, 276–279; and Ophuls, *Ecology and the Politics of Scarcity*, 39–40, 58–61.

27. Narveson, "Concept of Resources," 8.

28. See Reisner, *Cadillac Desert*, 334–336; Tregarthen, "Water in Colorado," 120; and Worster, *Rivers of Empire*, 312–316.

29. Reisner, *Cadillac Desert*, 61–96.

30. No one, including Narveson, considers seriously the possibility that, in the foreseeable future, we will find more water on this planet than we already know about. And despite the recent discovery of water on our Moon and other bodies circling the Sun, those supplies are simply beyond our reach. In short, if more water is to be made available to westerners, it will have to come from known terrestrial sources.

31. Reisner, *Cadillac Desert*, 260, 298–299, 335.

32. Quoted in Reisner, *Cadillac Desert*, 11.

33. Ibid.

34. Ibid., 486–489.

35. Ibid., 488.

36. Ibid., 491–492.

37. Luna Leopold, quoted in Reisner, *Cadillac Desert*, 491; see also Daniel W. Bromley, *Environment and Economy: Property Rights and Public Policy* (Oxford: Basil Blackwell, 1991), 8, 82, 162; and Ophuls, *Ecology and the Politics of Scarcity*, 167.

38. Anderson, "Introduction," xix.

39. See Daniel C. McCool, ed., *Command of the Waters: Iron Triangles, Federal Water Development, and Indian Water* (Tucson: University of Arizona Press, 1994), 224.

40. See William K. Stevens, "Water: Pushing the Limits of an Irreplaceable Resource," *New York Times*, 8 December 1998, B1.

41. See Ophuls, *Ecology and the Politics of Scarcity*, 53, 148.

42. Narveson, "Concept of Resources," 9.

43. See Tregarthen, "Water in Colorado," 128–129.

44. Such changes have not occurred in large part because the doctrine of prior appropriation, which dictates how and by whom Colorado River water is used, does not create the incentives for doing so. This doctrine is discussed in some detail in chapter 2.

45. Jan van Schilfgaarde, the former head of the Department of Agriculture's Salinity Control Laboratory, as quoted in Reisner, *Cadillac Desert*, 461–462.

46. See Reisner, *Cadillac Desert*, 459–460.

47. See Hundley, *Water and the West*, 315.

48. Ibid.; see also Worster, *Rivers of Empire*, 320–322.

49. See Carrier, Introduction to *The Colorado*; Reisner, *Cadillac Desert*, 460–461; and Worster, *Rivers of Empire*, 320–322.

50. See Hundley, *Water and the West*, 315.

51. Narveson, "Concept of Resources," 9.

52. The degradation would not be stopped entirely. The river would continue to get saltier because rainwater percolating through the ground on its way to the river would increase its salinity. This continued degradation would, however, be measurable only over the course of eons.

53. See Reisner, *Cadillac Desert*, 460–465.

54. Richard D. Lamm, "Depletion of Underground Water Foundation Imperils Vast Farming Region," *New York Times*, 11 August 1981, B4.

2

Water Rights Doctrines,
East and West

> Eventually, prior appropriation must give way to a new alloca-
> tion system that pays as much attention to protecting the physi-
> cal environment as to protecting vested rights, and to protecting
> common interests as well as individual needs. Nevertheless, in
> the 1990s prior appropriation remains the rule of law in most
> parts of the American West.
>
> Donald J. Pisani, *Water, Land, and Law in the West*

INTRODUCTION

The doctrine of prior appropriation, or "appropriationism," is the
rule of water law in the American West. Under that doctrine, the first
person to appropriate and put to use some quantity of water thereby
comes to have exclusive, secure, and transferable rights to it. The
only stipulation is that the water be put to some "beneficial use." As
will be discussed, the granting of such extensive property rights over
water to individuals—what amounts to a form of private property—
has been a direct cause of many of the problems that were outlined in
chapter 1. It is by virtue of having such rights that individuals can
continue to degrade and deplete the West's water, even though such
degradation and depletion is not in the best interests of the region as
a whole. In succeeding chapters, it is argued that the rights of indi-

viduals with regard to water in the West should be more limited, and that the extent and content of those rights should be shaped by a notion of "benefit" more closely connected to the collective wants and needs of westerners. The region's interests in conserving and sustaining its available water supply would be better served if water were jointly managed, such that an individual's interests are balanced against the community's interests as a whole. As will be discussed in chapter 3, where managerial powers are largely divorced from an individual's use rights, we have a common-property arrangement.

In the eastern part of the United States, a significantly different doctrine of water rights exists, one under which an individual's rights to use water are shaped by a "reasonable use" standard. "Reasonable" here is a relative notion, correlative with both the uses to which others can use the water and the interests of the larger community in which those water users live. As both uses and interests are subject to change, the rights of individual water users in the East are thereby rendered less secure than water rights in the West. The eastern doctrine of riparianism, with its notion of reasonable use, more closely resembles what we should strive for in the West, though there are aspects of it that we should not want to duplicate. In particular, the courts have been and continue to be largely responsible for shaping water law in the East. And as will be discussed, such an institution lacks the expertise and continuity needed to manage scarce water resources effectively.

In this chapter, I first examine the development and details of riparianism. And following that discussion, I examine the development and details of appropriationism. Riparianism is discussed first because it developed first: the western doctrine of prior appropriation "grew logically out of an adaptable common law and appeared in New England years before it developed in the West."[1] Riparianism developed as a particular response to the conditions and attitudes that arose in the East in the early part of the nineteenth century. Those same attitudes resulted in a different response in the West, where although the conditions were quite different than in the East, the process was nonetheless the same. The economist Harold Demsetz has argued that the emergence of property rights "takes place in response to the desires of the interacting persons for adjustment to new benefit-cost possibilities."[2] As a resource becomes scarce and therefore valuable, individuals attempt to better define their rights to that resource; property rights evolve in response to changing conditions and attitudes. In order to better understand and evaluate the evolution of property rights under appropriationism, then, it is helpful to first understand and evaluate its progenitor, and thereby come to see where a different evolutionary path may have led. Both attitudes and conditions in the West have changed since appropriationism was first developed. Rather than perpetuating the now-sour marriage of exclusive and secure property rights for water in the West, a different sort of rights-relationship should be allowed to develop, one that is better suited to water resources in the region.

RIPARIANISM

"Riparianism" is the name given to the doctrine of water rights that developed in New England in the early to middle part of the nineteenth century. Although in many cases it has since been augmented by a system of permits, riparianism remains the basis for water rights in most of the states east of the Mississippi River.[3] There are three main tenets of riparianism: (1) only individuals owning land along a river's course are entitled to use its water, (2) those individuals may use the water only on that land, and (3) those uses must be reasonable. The first tenet addresses who has rights to the water, the second addresses the extent of those rights, and the third addresses the content of those rights. The permit system has served to erode place-of-use restrictions, but the notion of reasonable use continues to be a primary feature of water rights in the East. And it is this notion that serves primarily to distinguish water rights in the East from those in the West, where temporal priority and beneficial use determine the extent and content of individuals' water rights.

Since my thesis is that western water rights should be based on a notion of reasonable use, it is important to understand how and why riparianism developed, and to comprehend as well the extent and content of water rights under that doctrine. After giving a brief account of how and why riparianism developed, I go on to discuss and evaluate the notion of reasonable use under that doctrine.

The Development of Riparianism

The term "riparian," used as an adjective, means "of, pertaining to, or situated or dwelling on the bank of a river or other body of water."[4] Thus, we can speak of riparian lands as those situated on the banks of a river, stream, lake, and so on. Alternatively, "riparian" can be used as a noun to refer to someone who owns land on the banks of a stream. A riparian right is one held by a riparian in virtue of his or her ownership of riparian land. A riparian right attaches to the land and is "as much a part of the soil as the stones scattered over it,"[5] such that if the riparian sells or otherwise loses title to his or her land, the riparian rights go along with the land. Nonriparians, of course, have no riparian rights.

Prior to the nineteenth century, the extent and content of riparian rights was defined not by what came to be known as riparianism, but rather by the natural flow doctrine. Under that doctrine, each riparian was entitled to have the stream flow through or by his or her land in its natural condition, "not materially retarded, diminished, or polluted by others."[6] That is, each riparian had a claim-right that the water continue to flow by his or her land in its natural state; or, we could say that each riparian had a right to consume water so long as the river was not noticeably diminished in either quantity or quality. The stream itself, its corpus, was thought to belong to no one in particular; it "belonged to everybody in general, belonged to God, belonged to itself."[7] Operationally, streams and rivers were considered a form of common property governed by rules specifying the rights of joint use. Each riparian had a right to use the water—a so-called usufructuary right, since no one owned the corpus of the stream itself—but only to the extent that such use did not materially alter the general condition of the watercourse. It did not matter if the riparian used the water in any productive sense: each riparian still had a claim-right to, if nothing else, sit on his or her veranda and contemplate the stream flowing by his or her land. Under the natural flow doctrine, then, each riparian had an usufructuary right to use the water, and that right was limited by the claim-rights of all other riparians along the same stream. Since all riparians had the same rights, there was a fundamental equality implied in the natural flow doctrine.

The natural flow doctrine was an expression of the view, dating from at least the time of Justinian, that nature should be left free to take its own course, and that running water was by its very nature common to all mankind. As the eighteenth-century English jurist William Blackstone put it, "For water is a moving, wandering thing, and must by necessity continue common by the law of nature; so that I can only have a temporary, transient, usufructuary property therein."[8] In a time when most land was used for agrarian purposes, and when such uses did not require either the transformation or consumptive use of flowing water, such rules proved generally adequate. In the humid climate of New England, water falling as precipitation sufficed for growing crops, and each town located away from a watercourse had a well for drinking water, so nonriparians were not materially inconvenienced by their lack of access to flowing water. Riparians themselves tended to use quite minimal amounts of river water, mostly for household purposes: bathing, drinking, gardening, and the like.[9] Because of the lack of tension and conflict among riparians living along the same stream, or between riparians and nonriparians, water rights under the natural flow doctrine were rarely in dispute. And when disputes did arise, the courts' decisions clearly and consistently expressed the prevailing doctrine. In a 1795 New Jersey case brought by a downstream riparian against an upstream riparian who was diverting water, the court said:

> In general it may be observed, when a man purchases a piece of land through which a natural water-course flows, he has a right to make use of it in its natural state, but not to stop or divert it to the prejudice of another. . . . The water flows in its natural channel, and ought always to be permitted to run there, so that all through whose land it pursues its natural course, may continue to enjoy the privilege of using it for their own purposes. It cannot legally be diverted from its course without the consent of all who have an interest in it.[10]

The demise of the natural flow doctrine and its gradual replacement by riparianism was engendered first and foremost by the dawning of a new economic order, under which nature came to be seen not as something to be left alone, but rather as just so many productive resources that could, and *should*, be exploited in the name of economic development. The idea that rivers and streams were to be left in their natural state was supplanted by "a dynamic, instrumental, and more abstract view that emphasized the newly paramount virtues of productive use."[11] Putting rivers to productive use in the early nineteenth century, through diversions and through the construction of relatively large dams and mills along streams, significantly altered the natural flow of rivers, and thereby created tension and conflict among riparians along a stream. The natural flow doctrine was clearly antidevelopmental: Any riparian could play dog in the manger, "not using the water but depriving upstream owners of its use by insisting on the maintenance of natural flow."[12] Yet just such development was coming to be the order of the day; it was increasingly coming to be embraced as politically and socially—that is, economically—desirable. Concomitant with judges' growing awareness at the time that "they were as equally responsible with legislation for governing society and promoting socially desirable conduct,"[13] the courts began to issue rulings that served to modify the received common law and adapt water rights to the dictates of the new economic order. In short, the content of water rights began to be justified in terms of their *utility in promoting economic development*.

In 1805, in the case of *Palmer v. Mulligan*, a court—in this case the New York Supreme Court—for the first time held that a riparian owner could obstruct the flow of water for mill purposes, ruling that the common law action for interference with the flow of water "must be restrained within reasonable bounds."[14] Over the next forty to fifty years, the productive capacity of New England mills increased sixfold, and judges and legal scholars continued to adapt the natural flow doctrine in order to better serve economic ends. More water rights cases were decided in this time than in the entire history of the common law.[15] By 1828, the prevailing view was that the natural flow doctrine "must not be construed literally, for that would be to deny all valuable use of the water to the riparian [since] rivers and streams of water would become utterly useless."[16] The transformation of the natural flow doctrine into what we now call riparianism is marked, then, by the increasing power of the idea that a rule of reasonable use was the proper test for determining the extent and content of water rights. This transformation did not happen overnight, but by midcentury it was largely complete.

The Rule of Reasonable Use

At the beginning of the nineteenth century, then, technological developments, the recognition that rivers and streams had economic value if the flow of water was materially altered, and the emergent social desirability of extracting the economic value of resources all served to uncover the antidevelopmental character of the natural flow doctrine. The doctrine's severe limitations on water use were, therefore, patently unacceptable to a society so oriented. And the courts, recognizing that the common law was both a malleable and acceptable vehicle for promoting socially desirable ends, began to modify the natural flow doctrine's rule—that no use was allowed that materially altered the flow of water—into the rule of reasonable use now associated with riparianism. But what, exactly, is a reasonable use, and how does such a notion affect the extent and content of riparians' rights? What the *Palmer* court meant by "reasonable" was not spelled out—the New York court justified its break with past doctrine by arguing that the injury to the lower riparian was only slight—but it was clear that "reasonable" had something to do with productive use. By 1844, in the Massachusetts Supreme Court case of *Cary v. Daniels*, it had become somewhat clearer what the courts took "reasonable" to mean. Chief Justice Lemuel Shaw said that it meant "a use profitable to the [riparian] owner, and beneficial to the public"; this, though, was to be weighed against the additional requirements that one could neither "wholly destroy or divert" a stream so as to prevent the water from flowing to a downstream riparian, nor "wholly obstruct" it to the disadvantage of one upstream.[17] That is, a riparian could neither divert so much water that a downstream mill owner's operations were adversely affected, nor could a riparian build a dam that raised the water level to such an extent that an upstream mill was materially disadvantaged. Such a ruling, however, left plenty of room for judicial interpretation and manipulation. A mill owner who did not "wholly" obstruct a stream, for instance, might claim that since his operation both contributed more to the community than did his upstream competitor's and was more profitable to himself, the needs and wants of the community, as well as his own benefits, justified *some* diminution to his competitor's operation.

What finally emerges from these and other courts' decisions is that whether a use is reasonable or not is a question of fact to be determined by the courts on a case-by-case basis using a multifactor test:

> The factors that affect this judicial determination are: (1) the purpose of the use; (2) the suitability of the use to the watercourse; (3) the economic value of the use; (4) the social value of the use; (5) the extent and amount of harm it causes; (6) the practicality of avoiding the harm by adjusting the use or method of use of one proprietor or the other; (7) the practicality of adjusting the quantity of water used by each proprietor; (8) the protection of existing values of water uses, land, investments and enterprises; and (9) the justice of requiring the user causing harm to bear the loss.[18]

First, we should notice that gone from this list of factors is the notion that the "natural state" of a watercourse is in any sense sacrosanct. Maintaining fish or fowl habitats, a river's navigability, or even a public recreational site might readily be considered of pressing social or public value and thus be protected by the courts. More generally, such considerations concern the second factor, the suitability of a use, and might well be used to justify maintaining some *minimal flow level*. For example, a huge mill on a tiny stream might not be deemed suitable, but only if other factors do not indicate otherwise. If the profit to the proprietor and the value to the public are great enough, then the court *could* rule that not even a minimal flow needs to be maintained. But the history of riparianism in the East shows that the courts have generally protected minimal flows.[19]

Gone, too, is the idea that sitting on one's veranda and contemplating the river flowing by is, in and of itself, a right to be protected. If the market value of the land is decreased because of the diminution of flow, then *that* might be a telling factor, but idle contemplation is not an activity considered to be of economic value. Aesthetic values qua social values *might* be taken into consideration, of course, although it does not appear that they were until quite recently. But the claim-rights of individual riparians are now almost exclusively based on economic factors: by and large, only riparians engaged in productive activities have a basis for claiming water rights. If two riparians, Farmer and Miller, both acquired riparian land in the eighteenth century, then both originally had claim-rights against the other that the flow of water not be materially changed simply in virtue of each one's ownership of riparian land. Let us further stipulate that Farmer's land is directly upstream from Miller's. If in 1845 Farmer is able to divert water onto his land and thereby produce prodigious amounts of corn, and if Miller uses her land only for weekend retreats from the city, then all else being equal, Miller would no longer have a claim-right to the unimpeded flow of the stream. Whereas there was a fundamental equality implied in the natural flow doctrine, the notion of reasonable *economic* use eroded such equality by valuing economic development above equal access.

Looking at the factors to be considered by the courts, it is also clear that, under riparianism, every riparian has a right to use water for any purpose *if the use is reasonable with respect to other riparians*, that is, if the use does not unreasonably interfere with other riparians' legitimate uses. Diversion rights under riparianism are thus said to be correlative rights: "mutually interdependent and not merely based on benefit to a single user."[20] So, in suits between two riparians, both riparians' uses are at issue. Rivers and streams, then, were still considered common property, and the existing rights of one riparian could be affected by the actions of another. Continuing with the previous example, suppose that in 1850 Miller dams the stream in order to run a mill that processes corn. Damming the stream creates a lake adjacent to Farmer's land that attracts large numbers of animals, which are attracted to the corn Farmer grows, and the foraging animals subsequently ravage Farmer's corn crop. If milling corn is now more valuable to the community than growing it, then, all else being equal, the rule of reasonable use might well cause the courts to deny Farmer's suit for damages to his crops. Even if both uses are of equal value to both the individuals and the community, the now-abundant wildlife might afford a windfall to the area in terms of fresh meat, and the courts could decide on this basis that Miller's activities were preferred over Farmer's. Again, economic considerations are put above considerations of equal access. And if the relative utility of one activity were greater than that of another, then it would be consistent to assign water use rights to whomever could get the most value from the water. If both Miller *and* the community now get more value from the water than does Farmer, then, in terms of utility, Miller should get to use the water.

The inclusion of the eighth factor, the protection of existing values of water uses, makes it clear that one consideration for assigning water rights under riparianism is the temporal priority of productive water use: all else being equal, first in time is first in right. If Miller, who is downstream from Farmer, began diverting water before Farmer did, then Miller thereby acquires a claim-right against Farmer that he not reduce the flow of the stream so as to adversely impact her. Such a result was clearly intended in Chief Justice Shaw's decision in *Cary*: "[the] proprietor who first erects a dam ... has a right to maintain it, as against the proprietors above and below; and to this extent, *prior occupancy give a prior title to such use.*"[21]

At least in the early stages of technological development, such a priority rule obviously encourages economic development: Miller will only invest time and capital in growing corn if her rights to the water are fairly secure. If she believes that her rights to the water could be easily lost, then such uncertainty will preclude her investment. Yet in an era of constantly changing technology, as the early nineteenth century was, the price to be paid for securing rights to the first developer was that future advancements and efficiencies could not be realized. If Farmer could make better use of the water—either by growing corn more efficiently or by putting the water to some other use entirely—but such use would adversely impact Miller's prior use, then a strict adherence to a rule of prior development was inconsistent with the dictates of utility. The sanctity of rights, then, is here again, as it was previously, at odds with the dictates of utility: the former affords *security* to the rights holder, whereas the latter allows greater *flexibility* and economic gain for the community.

In the end, eastern courts rejected security in favor of flexibility, not only because such security was bought at the price of foregoing greater economic gain, but also because vesting rights in the first appropriator was thought to lead to monopoly, and monopoly was seen as depriving the public "of the benefit which always attends competition and rivalry."[22] Priority of use is still a factor in determining reasonable use under riparianism, but only where all the other factors even out. For the most part, the riparian doctrine, both in theory and practice, "allows entry of new users and requires old users to accommodate them.... [T]he relationship among present and future riparian uses on a particular watercourse is one of parity rather than priority."[23] But what should be kept in mind for when the discussion turns to appropriationism is that the concept of "first in time, first in right" is not unique to that doctrine.

An Evaluation of Riparianism

Under riparianism, rights to use water from a watercourse extend only to riparians and their riparian lands. The basis and content of these rights depends on the use to which that water is put. The security of this claim-right, however, is rather tenuous, because it concerns the reasonableness of a riparian's use vis-à-vis all other riparians along the same watercourse. The courts have been the primary determinant of what constitutes reasonable use; and what has tended to be deemed most reasonable by the courts has, in large measure, been a matter of which use is considered the most economically productive.

If we accept the fact that water rights should be allocated to those who can use that water most productively or efficiently, then why should we limit the extent of those rights only to riparian lands? Such place-of-use restrictions originated in a time and place— preindustrial England—where only lands immediately adjacent to watercourses could be the sites of viable water uses. But there is no necessary correlation between contiguity of land and water and the ability to benefit from using the water, as is demonstrated by the development of technology to economically divert large amounts of water to nonriparian lands.

In explaining the variety of rules by which someone can legitimately acquire property rights in or ownership of some thing, David Hume, writing in the 1740s, cites both "use" and "accession" as being among the relevant considerations. According to Hume, first and foremost someone should "continue to enjoy what he is at present possess'd of," and by "possess'd of" Hume means that we "have it in our power to use it."[24] That Miller is using some amount of water now is a good, though not incontestable, reason for assigning property rights to that water to Miller. One acquires something W by accession when that person already owns something closely connected to W, "Thus the fruits of our garden [and] the offspring of our cattle [are] esteem'd our property."[25] That is, our untutored imagination, within certain bounds, naturally associates things contiguous to what a person already owns with that person. And it is through accession alone, states Hume, that "the property of rivers, by the laws of most nations, and by *the natural turn of our thought*, is attributed to the proprietors of their banks."[26] But accession is a more tenuous reason than is use for assigning ownership of some object to some person, because in the end, Hume thinks, it is the usefulness of a rule to society's well being that ultimately holds sway: "Public utility," he writes elsewhere, "is the general object of all courts of judicature."[27] Where determining property via accession is not conducive to public utility, the dictates of utility will, Hume believes, eventually overbalance the conclusions of our untutored imagination. If Farmer claims use rights based solely on the contiguity of his land to the river, and Smith claims use rights based on her ability to put the water to productive use, even though her land is nonriparian, we should expect that, eventually, the law will decide in Smith's favor as considerations of public utility come to dominate society's thoughts.

The case against limiting the extent of water rights to riparian lands where productivity and efficiency are paramount considerations is strengthened if we consider that individuals originally settled riparian lands without much regard to the productive capacity of the flowing water. As was pointed out earlier, until the nineteenth century the natural flow doctrine inconvenienced neither riparians nor nonriparians. The fact is that both conditions and attitudes changed and thereby delivered a windfall to riparians; now, riparians' claim-rights to the water were potentially much more valuable. If a riparian could not use the water flowing by his or her land, then by selling that use right to a nonriparian, both parties could benefit. However, by restricting water use to riparian lands, and thereby limiting the transferability of the use right, riparianism serves to reduce the possible benefits of water use.

Again, Hume is instructive here. Believing that the first establishment of property depends "very much on chance" and is "a grand inconvenience, which calls for a remedy," Hume thinks that rules allowing for the "adjustment of property to persons" will inevitably develop because such adjustments are "determin'd by a plain utility and interest." The rules of "mutual exchange and commerce" that best adjust property to persons constitute an open market.[28] Regardless of by which rule or rules someone came originally to have property in a thing—use, accession, and so on—utility would be better served if all property were susceptible to free exchange. Restricting such free exchange of property hampers the process whereby the ownership of productive resources is adjusted to better reflect an individual's wants and desires. If utility is what you are after, then restricting the distribution of water use rights for other than utilitarian reasons is antithetical.

As was discussed earlier, the lack of security in water rights under riparianism is another impediment to maximizing the possible benefits of water use. Technology requires investment, and one inducement for investment is the relative certainty that that investment will not be lost through the vicissitudes of other riparians' changing attitudes and uses. Of course, one major inducement for technological improvement is the ability to profit from that improvement, so that the same rationale used by an early innovator—"I should have a claim-right to use water because my use is more reasonable than hers"—can similarly be invoked by a later innovator to trump the rights of the earlier user. As long as consequentialist considerations are foremost, this tension between the security and flexibility of water rights will not abate, because what is considered reasonable is not a fixed standard. This is true even if we replace "maximizing economic benefit" with something else, like "conserving and sustaining resource quality," for such a goal might also require adjusting an individual's rights as the quality of the resource deteriorates. Regardless of the particular goal, what appears reasonable today might well become unreasonable in the future. Property rights under utilitarian theories of property are inherently unstable.[29] If we must live with a situation in which, because of this or that goal, an individual's rights are never totally secure, then the justice of curtailing or revoking an individual's rights to use water vis-à-vis that goal will remain an open possibility.

Given this possibility, the *process* by which reasonableness is determined becomes of paramount concern. That is, if we accept the fact that there are valid reasons for revoking an individual's water rights, then the reasonableness of how and by whom that nullification occurs is itself brought into sharper focus. One of the major criticisms of riparianism is that the process by which reasonable use is determined under that doctrine is simply unpalatable: "allocation decisions in pure riparian states are made by the courts, an institution lacking the expertise and administrative *continuity* to assure a predictable diversion rights system. Case-by-case judicial decision making results in *inconsistent* and impermanent results."[30] Impermanence is perhaps ineliminable, as I have previously suggested, but achieving more consistency and continuity in the process are legitimate goals. One option would be to create a single, centralized agency, as some have suggested.[31] There are, however, other, more palatable avenues for achieving more consistency and continuity in determining reasonable use, as will be discussed in chapter 6. My purpose here is to point out that insofar as achieving consistency and continuity in the process of determining reasonableness are legitimate goals, the judicial, case-by-case process of riparianism is open to reproach.

The previous criticisms—the anachronistic and somewhat arbitrary assignment of water rights to riparians, as well as the inconsistency and discontinuity of judicial authority—have led fifteen of the twenty-five eastern riparian-rule states to enact administrative permit systems that allow for the management and allocation of water substantially independent of the riparian system. Although there is much variability from state to state, the permit systems generally allow both riparians and nonriparians to apply for water use permits, and such permits are issued for fixed terms, ranging anywhere from ten to fifty years, thus adding a measure of security to the permitees' investments. In addition, such permits are usually transferable, though there are some restrictions on both the place and purpose of water use for those buying permits from permitees. In short, the permit system, where it has been implemented, has served to rectify many of the more objectionable aspects of riparianism.[32]

What remains intact, though, and what distinguishes eastern water rights doctrines from western ones, is that *who* can use water from a watercourse and *how* that water is used are subject to considerations of reasonableness that, in the broadest terms, concern the social value of that use. Historically, what has been of value to society has been extracting the most economic value from the available resources. But that attitude is no longer sacrosanct. Our values have broadened and changed concomitant with the depletion and degradation of water resources. It is no longer just of concern to riparians what happens to a river; the protection of public access rights and the maintenance of fish and wildlife habitat are among the broader, noneconomic social interests now taken into consideration by the courts and administrative agencies. The notion of reasonable use is flexible and expandable enough to encompass such values, which is its primary virtue. Whether use rights are extended to nonriparians, whether such rights are vested for predictable but limited periods of time, whether the courts or another political body is the primary vehicle for such determinations, the fact that such determinations are subject to considerations beyond the economic value of a particular water use to a particular individual is the feature of eastern water rights that is sorely lacking in the West. It is to an examination of the western doctrine of prior appropriation that I now turn.

PRIOR APPROPRIATION

Prior appropriation, or appropriationism, is the doctrine of water rights that developed in the western United States in the mid to late nineteenth century. While some western states employ a blended doctrine that employs features of both the riparian and the prior appropriation doctrines, the doctrine of prior appropriation is generally regarded as governing the control and use of surface water in the seventeen states west of the Mississippi.[33]

There are two central features or principles of appropriationism. The basic principle is: *"qui prior est in tempore, potior est in jure"*— who is first in time, is first in right.[34] The first person that diverts and puts to use some amount of water thereby gains an exclusive right to that quantity of water; the rights of later appropriators may not interfere with the rights of those who have preceded them.[35] After priority in time, the second major principle is that "beneficial use shall be the basis, measure, and limit to the use of water."[36] Although statutes identify some beneficial uses, what counts as a beneficial use is, as with reasonable use under riparianism, largely operational, and must be tested in each case. Historically, what uses have been considered beneficial are those that are of economic value to individual appropriators.

As with riparianism, I will first give a brief account of how and why appropriationism developed. I go on to compare the extent and content of water rights under appropriationism with those under riparianism, and then evaluate the doctrine of prior appropriation with a view back toward the previous discussion in chapter 1.

The Development of Prior Appropriation

Unlike those who originally settled in the East, those who settled the West were never attached to the view that nature should be left free to take its own course. They were enthralled from the start with the "new capitalist economic culture and its attitudes toward nature."[37] They believed that it was not only their right, but also their duty to exploit nature to the fullest in the name of economic development. The eastern doctrine of riparianism fit neither the needs nor the situation of the first Anglo settlers of the West, those miners who, in the late 1840s, came to California in search of gold.[38] Rather, what emerged "gradually, amidst conflict, as a response to the rise of the private corporation and to new techniques of mining" was the doctrine of prior appropriation.[39] Agriculture ultimately supplanted mining in the 1860s as the basis for the region's economy, but western courts and legislatures simply extended prior appropriation to agriculture by applying questionable precedents culled from earlier mining cases. And by 1900, prior appropriation was firmly fastened on the West.

In the baldest terms, the early miners simply took and appropriated what they needed. Although they were essentially squatting on land that was still in the public domain,[40] the territorial, state, and federal governments had vested interests in the miners being there—their swelling ranks were a form of political security, and the minerals they extracted served to swell political coffers—and the authorities therefore turned a blind eye to the strict illegality of the miners' activities. Water was an integral part of those activities. Either streams had to be diverted in order to get at the placer deposits in those stream beds, or they had to be diverted in order to wash away top soil and expose dry, ancient stream beds. As placer deposits were exhausted and hydraulic guns began to be employed, the value of diverting the water increased dramatically, and it was diverted farther and farther away from its natural course.[41]

The miners felt justified in their actions because, as far as they were concerned, there were no prior claims on either the land or the water. We should remember that when flowing water became valuable in the East in the early 1800s, it was already considered a form of common property. Individuals by and large already owned the banks of watercourses, and each riparian had a claim-right against all others that they not interfere with the flow of the river. Under either a riparian or a permit system, rights to water in the East are still subject to a complex set of rules specifying rights of joint use. When Anglo settlers first came to the West, however, both the land and the water were, in theory, owned by the government, though it had not actually asserted property rights for either one.[42] Since there were, in practice, no existing claim-rights, western land and water were treated by the miners as *res nullius*—literally "no one's property." As such, both land and water were not thought of as common property; rather, they were considered open-access resources, meaning resources over which no property rights had been recognized.[43] Since they felt they had no duties to anyone to refrain from doing so, the miners simply took and used whatever they needed. The government legitimated the miners' activities, at first by not taking any action to thwart the miners' appropriations, and eventually by honoring those appropriations through court and legislative decisions. In 1855, the California Supreme Court proclaimed that its duty was to "foster and protect the mining interests as paramount to all others."[44] And protecting the mining interests meant officially legitimating the doctrine of water rights the miners had worked out among themselves in the mining camps. First the miners, needing water for their sluice boxes, simply took it without a second thought. Once this became an established practice, and since the states had essentially encouraged it, the lawmakers had little choice but to honor these rights. In short, first use came to be regarded as conferring property rights in water.[45]

Over time and by common agreement, what the miners worked out among themselves was that temporal priority in appropriating (i.e., putting to use) an amount of water conferred an absolute right to that water. It did not matter if one miner's claim proved more valuable than another's: as long as there was at least a modicum of wealth being produced, a miner's water rights were respected by others. Such rights could, however, be lost through nonuse. In order to ensure that no valuable mineral rights were wasted, local custom sanctioned claim jumping—seizing another miner's territory— whenever "the prior claimant had abandoned his claim [or] had failed to diligently work it."[46] Since an individual's claim-rights to the water were recognized and honored by others in virtue of the productive use to which that individual put it, failure to continue using the water constituted losing all claim-rights to the water as well. If an individual sold his actively worked mining claim, then the water rights passed to the new owner and retained their same temporal priority, or seniority.[47] The water rights of claim jumpers, however, were considered "new" rights, that is, honored only insofar as temporally prior, or senior, appropriators were not injured. "Whatever changes occurred in the doctrine of prior appropriation as it spread from mining to agriculture, two principles remained inviolable: that chronological priority of a use transcended the value of a use, and that rights to water were exclusive and absolute."[48]

A systematic account of the process by which the arid and semiarid regions of the West were settled by farmers from the 1860s through the turn of the century would show that appropriationism came to be the law of the land neither immediately nor without controversy. Indeed, the same would be true if one looked in detail at the development of prior appropriation in the mining camps. And as was indicated earlier, not all western states uniformly adopted appropriationism; some settled on riparianism, some on a blended doctrine. But in eight most-arid states (Colorado, Arizona, Idaho, Montana, Nevada, New Mexico, Utah, and Wyoming), riparianism was ignored entirely while appropriationism was recognized as the exclusive means by which the right to divert water could be acquired. It is generally acknowledged that such rules were basically culled from the mining camps and applied to agricultural and other uses of water in those states.[49]

The unsystematic and basic story is this: Mining proved an ephemeral fascination and false salvation for the West, and when the flow of precious minerals dried up in the late 1850s, the miners left. More security and long-term prosperity were promised for the region if large numbers of farmers could be enticed to come and permanently settle the land. The enticement came in the form of a series of state and federal statutes, passed from 1860 to 1877, that gave farmers ownership of land in the public domain if they could put that land to productive use. In the arid and semiarid regions of the West, dry-land farming was impossible. Growing crops in the region required irrigating them, which in turn required diverting large amounts of water. The infrastructure of dams and canals needed for irrigation required large capital investments, which would not be made unless those investors' rights to the water were firmly secured. As was discussed earlier, riparianism offered no such security, because under that doctrine claim-rights to water were subject to a variable reasonable use standard. The doctrine that developed in the mining camps, however, did offer such security, because water rights, once secured and continually used, were thereby rendered inviolable. Thus, the doctrine of prior appropriation was adopted because it provided economic incentives and opportunities for investors in irrigation projects. In 1876, the drafters of the Colorado constitution not only confirmed and protected existing appropriation claims, they also restricted all future rights to appropriative ones. And in 1877, Congress passed the Desert Lands Act, which specified that water used on public lands deeded to individuals be restricted to "bona-fide prior appropriation."[50]

In the relatively close-knit mining camps, a crude system of notice was sufficient in most cases for determining both how much water each miner was using and when such use began. As more and more farmers (and, eventually, manufacturers, power companies, and cities) diverted more and more water from more and more water-courses, disputes about such matters inevitably arose. In response, most states where prior appropriation was the rule eventually adopted water codes. Although the details of such codes were not uniform, they generally governed the approval of water appropriations, the determination and adjudication of conflicting claims, and the administration and distribution of water. The approval and adjudication process was often facilitated by a permit system; those who wished to divert water had to apply for a permit, which had to be approved before such diversion could begin. However, unlike eastern permit systems that served to modify riparianism, the water codes and permit systems in prior appropriation states were designed, and functioned, to more effectively administer the existing system: "The basic purpose behind these modifications was to enhance the operational efficiency of the original doctrine."[51]

In summary, in the arid regions of the West, temporal priority of water use—not efficiency or other considerations of justice—came to be, and remains, the primary determinant of who receives water and who does not. The only stipulation is that the water continues to be put to some profitable or wealth-producing use by the right holder.

Appropriationism versus Riparianism

Before evaluating appropriationism, it will be instructive at this point to compare the extent and content of water rights under appropriationism with those under riparianism. The sum of the differences between the two doctrines amounts to two different forms of property, a subject that will be taken up in greater detail in the next chapter.

First, since under appropriationism water rights are based on priority of beneficial use and not ownership of riparian land, theoretically, anyone can acquire rights to use water at any location. Practically speaking, appropriative rights are limited in extent only by the technical and economic limits of applying water from a particular source to use in a particular place. Where permit systems have been implemented in riparian-rule states, this difference is not so pronounced. Still, even in eastern permit states, nonriparians' uses of water are largely restricted to intrabasin locations, that is, where runoff flows back toward the originating source.[52] There are no such place-of-use restrictions under appropriationism. For example, the Grand Ditch, near Rocky Mountain National Park in Colorado, annually diverts twenty thousand acre-feet of water out of the Colorado River basin and across the Continental Divide.[53]

Second, an appropriative right exists for a definite quantity of water, and the right to use that water cannot be overridden by either junior appropriators' claims of better utilization of it or the community's claim of a more reasonable use for it. One consequence of this is that in times of shortage, a senior appropriator, if he or she is able to divert and use all the water he or she has rights to, can literally drain a watercourse bone-dry without regard to junior appropriators' rights. Suppose two individuals, Senior and Junior, both have claim-rights and are using some amount of water from a watercourse for irrigating corn; they live in Colorado, and Senior's claim is senior to Junior's. At such times when there is not enough water for both Senior and Junior to use their full appropriation, Senior need not share the burden of shortage with Junior. It does not matter whether Senior's diversion and use is upstream or downstream from Junior's, nor does it matter whether Senior's use is five miles away from the river. When there is not enough water for all users, a senior appropriator has the right to "take water from a junior appropriator below him, while the junior appropriator must permit the water to flow past his headgate if needed by a downstream senior."[54]

This situation contrasts sharply with riparianism, where the mutual interdependence or correlative nature of an individual's water rights means that, in times of shortage, the burden would be shared among those using water from the same watercourse. If we examine again the nine-factor test used to determine reasonable use under riparianism, we see that latecomers such as Junior could be allowed to continue to appropriate water—or even expropriate water from people like Senior—for all sorts of reasons: if the extent and amount of harm caused to Junior was worse than the harm caused to Senior; if the harm could be avoided if Senior simply repaired his leaky pipes; if it was practical for Senior to switch to a more efficient irrigation system; if Senior could adjust his use without unduly suffering; or if Junior's use protected the existing values of the watercourse, whether those values were purely economic or were otherwise considered socially desirable. Senior appropriators under riparianism hold no special status. Even the first appropriator's claim-rights are mutually interdependent with the claim-rights of all others.

A third difference, and one that follows from the two just discussed, is that since the content of appropriative rights are for *diverting* and *using* a definite amount of water, and since such rights are unconnected to the land, both how and where water is used by an

appropriator are subject to change. Even under eastern permit systems, permits are issued for a particular use at a particular location;
change of either requires approval of a new permit. Under
appropriationism, however, the present right holder is legally entitled to change both the nature and place of use, and, for that matter,
change the point of diversion or method of diversion.[55] He or she can
also sell or lease the right to use the water. In short, water rights are
almost entirely transferable under appropriationism, transferable
to either other uses or other users. The flexibility and marketability
of water rights under appropriationism makes them much more
valuable than under riparianism.

A fourth and final difference between the two doctrines is that an
appropriative water right is of an indefinite duration; it lasts for as
long as the water continues to be used for a beneficial purpose. Since
the right was established and exists because of actual use, the right
can be lost only through nonuse: use it, or lose it. "Should a rightholder
not use his right, or part of it, for a statutory period of time, and intend
not to use it, his water right may be lost through abandonment in a
proceeding brought by the state or a junior appropriator. Intent is
the key to abandonment."[56] We should remember that a riparian,
like Miller, can obtain a claim-right to water even if he or she does not
assert that right for a hundred years if his or her proposed use is
deemed more reasonable than some other established use. And if a
permitee in the East obtains a permit for fifty years for a particular
water use at a particular location, he or she does not lose his or her
rights, even if he or she never actually diverts and uses any water over
those fifty years. In the West, however, the scarcity of water and its necessity for extracting value from the land have made the existence of
rights to water conditional on diverting it and using it productively.

The content of water rights under both appropriationism and
riparianism consists of use rights, or usufructuary rights, only. One
who uses water, either in the East or in the West, does not thereby
come to own the corpus of the water; rather, that individual has the
right to the advantages of its use rather than to the fluid itself. In the
next chapter, I discuss in more detail the nature of a use right and its
status as a property right. But I should note here that the exclusivity,
security, and transferability of water use rights under appropriationism are so different in character than water use rights under
riparianism that the two doctrines constitute two different forms of
ownership. In the East, Miller's water use rights are for a particular
use at a particular location, and such rights can be either modified or
lost altogether though the actions and desires of others. In the West,

Senior's water use rights are for a particular *quantity* of water, to be used in virtually any manner or location he chooses. Senior can sell those rights, but priority issues aside, he cannot lose them save by failing to exercise them.

An Evaluation of Appropriationism

Under appropriationism, anyone can acquire the right to use water from a watercourse. That right is obtained by appropriating and putting to use some quantity of that water; the exercise of that right is limited only by the rights of prior appropriators; and the right is neither correlative with nor mutually interdependent on either other uses or other users that may come along in the future. That right is for a definite quantity of water, which can be freely transferred to other uses or other users; and that right is secured for an indefinite duration, that is, for as long as the water continues to be put to some actual, productive, wealth-producing use.

The primary defect of appropriationism is the result of its primary virtue: the absolute security of a right held by a senior appropriator to use a definite quantity of water. As was discussed earlier, such security came to be legitimized as an economic incentive to attract settlers and investment in irrigation projects. Such an incentive operated, in turn, on the belief that was almost universal in late nineteenth-century America, "that the West should be building up its population and growing crops, [and] that its water or any other resource should be exploited to its maximum economic potential."[57] As a tool for providing incentives and opportunities for the initial economic development of the West, guaranteeing the security of water rights seemed to make good sense: "how better to develop an economy than initially to provide the first developers with guarantees against future competitive injury?"[58] But as a tool for parceling out a scarce resource, securing nearly absolute rights to the first appropriators for a definite quantity of water is grossly inefficient. It discourages improvements in irrigation and serves to perpetuate other wasteful practices.

In the West in the late nineteenth century, hydrology was in its infancy, and farmers, assuming more water was better than less, tended to appropriate more of it than they actually needed for their particular use. Comprehensive studies of the optimum amount of water required for different soils and crops did not begin until the late 1890s. Early diversion ditches were poorly constructed and maintained, almost guaranteeing that much diverted water was being wasted through seepage and evaporation; it was not until the early 1900s that extensive studies were made on the optimum design for diversion ditches.[59] But since beneficial use does not mean efficient, reasonable, or economical use, early appropriators maintained their rights to the original quantity of water they diverted. As long as they had some wealth-producing use for the water they used, they could claim a beneficial use, and their rights to a definite amount of water were, and are, secured.

Suppose Senior and Junior are both growing corn. As long as there is enough water for Senior to use his entire appropriation, he has little incentive to upgrade his irrigation ditch, repair his leaky pipes, or switch from flood to drip irrigation.[60] The burden of any shortage would first be entirely borne by Junior. If Senior were to improve the efficiency of his water use and thereby reduce the amount of water he was diverting and using, he would eventually, by failing to either use it or to have an intention of using it, simply lose rights to that "saved" water. It would be available for appropriation by others, and Senior would receive no compensation for his loss.[61] Although it would be more efficient if Senior changed his ways, his inability to capture the benefits of doing so reduces the chances that such changes will occur.

If we suppose further that Junior, after experiencing a few shortages, does switch to drip irrigation, while Senior continues his wasteful practices, blissfully unmindful of Junior's efforts, we begin to feel that some injustice has been worked if Junior is still not able to use any water because of a shortage. Some of our most powerful intuitions tell us that there is something either mildly unpalatable or simply wrong with not making *some* demands on Senior if Junior, after all her efforts, still cannot get the water she needs. This feeling is especially pronounced if Senior only needs to make some minimal effort in order to greatly improve Junior's situation. This sense of unfairness, however, might not warrant taking any action against Senior. Because Senior has existing rights, and because we also have intuitions that suggest that respecting existing rights is important too, we would have to show that the unfairness of the situation outweighed or trumped the sanctity of an individual's rights.[62] Our inability to persuade or coerce Senior into making what seem like reasonable modifications to his operation not only results in inefficient use of water—more water would be available if Senior changed his ways—but also seems intuitively unfair: certainly Junior deserves something for her efforts.

Securing rights to a fixed quantity of water also perpetuates other wasteful practices. A senior appropriator, we should remember, could be irrigating crops many miles away from a watercourse. It costs money to build and maintain long irrigation ditches; seepage and evaporation increase in proportion to the distance diverted; return flows decrease in similar proportion; and soil outside of alluvial basins tends to be less productive than soil adjoining rivers and streams. It would cost less money and waste less water if farmers whose lands were closer to the watercourse used the water to irrigate their crops instead. It would benefit the community in absolute terms if water were applied in this more reasonable fashion: more farmers could cultivate more crops on more land, resulting in benefits for (almost) everyone. But as long as Senior is producing some wealth for himself through his application of water, he is permitted to continue to divert as much water as he has a right to use, regardless of whether others' uses are more reasonable than his.

Since location along a watercourse is largely irrelevant under appropriationism, shortages might require upstream junior appropriators to let water flow by their diversion ditches so downstream seniors can use their full allotment. This practice, too, can result in much waste. For example, in a 1940 Nebraska Supreme Court case,[63] the court ruled that an upstream junior appropriator along the North Platte River had to stop her diversions altogether so that a downstream senior appropriator could receive usable quantities of water. These were the only two water users along this stretch of the river. Losses due to evaporation are heavy along the North Platte, due to the shallow and wide character of the watercourse. Senior had rights to 162 cubic-feet of water, but in order for that much water to be delivered to Senior, 700 cubic-feet of water had to be in the river just beyond Junior's diversion point. That is, between Junior's and Senior's locations, two-thirds of the river's flow was lost to evaporation and seepage, and often there was less than seven hundred cubic-feet left in the river when it flowed by Junior's land. Obviously, much less water would be wasted if Junior were allowed to divert and use at least some water. The court, however, held that "although the losses suffered in doing so are great," if delivery of a usable quantity of water can be made to Senior, it must be allowed: "To permit the officers of the state the right to say whether prospective losses would or would not justify the delivery of usable quantities of water would clothe such officers with a discretion incompatible with the vested interests of the realtors, and destroy the very purpose of the doctrine of appropriation existent in this state."[64] In addition to undermining the economic potential of the available water, such a decision goes

against our intuition, discussed earlier, that in times of scarcity the
sanctity of rights should be subject to some abridgement.

Not only does appropriationism lack sufficient incentives to discourage inefficient and wasteful water uses, it also has not easily ac-
commodated "new uses." If we consider that in this century water
has attained value for, among other things, recreation, scenic or aesthetic beauty, and ecological protection, we see that the notion of beneficial use under appropriationism must be expanded in order for
such new uses to be recognized. There is a pronounced if not exclusive emphasis on the fact that "beneficial" means economically *valuable* (though as was just discussed, this does *not* mean economically
efficient). Also, using water has tended to require diverting it from a
watercourse. But in most cases the new uses are in-stream uses, and
neither recreation, nor scenic beauty, nor ecological protection have
to be economically valuable; in most cases, they are probably not. In
several western states, statutes have been passed that specifically
classify in-stream uses as legitimate uses, and specify noneconomic
values as beneficial ones. Where such statutes have been passed,
both their scope and meaning have been challenged in the courts. In
all such cases, the statutes themselves were seen as modifications to
appropriationism, even if the court ultimately accepted those modifications.[65] Insofar as such new uses have come to be accepted, then,
they have done so only through a modification of beneficial use as
originally conceived of under appropriationism.

But even where such new uses have gained acceptance, their future is far from secure. First, water for such uses is still considered
an appropriation.[66] Since senior appropriators can take their full
share first, and since appropriations for new uses tend to be very junior ones, in times of shortage the new uses will be the first ones
stopped. Second, some states have passed statutes that identify preferred uses, meaning those deemed to be more beneficial than other
ones. In times of shortage, a preferred use "may condemn a nonpre-
ferred use in order to supply a *higher* use, regardless of temporal priority of diversion."[67] This, too, marks a departure from the two basic
tenets of appropriationism. As originally conceived, appropriationism
made no distinction between classes of beneficial uses. Nevertheless,
the ranking of preferred uses in the states where such rankings have
been made and upheld still favor economic uses over noneconomic
ones. Normally, the ranking of uses is: domestic uses; agricultural
uses; industrial and power uses; and fish, wildlife, and recreational
uses. So, even where appropriations for new uses are senior to appro-

priations for other traditional uses, the law dictates that in times of shortage such new uses would suffer first.

In addition to perpetuating wasteful practices and discriminating against new uses, securing rights to senior appropriators for a definite quantity of water also ignores issues of water quality. As was discussed in chapter 1, as water is diverted, used, and returned to the watercourse over and over again, its quality deteriorates both over time and as one moves downstream. This deterioration is due mostly to an increase in salinity. The increasing salinity means that a downstream appropriator, even the most senior one, must, if he is to continue to use water in the same way, either purchase more water from another appropriator or invest in water-purification and irrigation technology. Either option, if even available, would be costly. Moreover, either option constitutes a response to the *symptoms* of deteriorating water quality, and not to its *causes*; such options are only stopgap measures.

It would be more reasonable, both in terms of the costs and the long-term sustainability of the resource, to try to curtail the degradation of the quality of the water in the first place rather than to try to deal with it after the fact. For instance, the less water that is diverted and applied to crops, and the less distance that water has to percolate back through salt-rich soils, the less salt will be picked up and washed back into the watercourse. This implies that water quality deterioration could be curtailed if porous irrigation works were repaired, if diversion rights were better coordinated with actual amounts needed, if alluvial lands were better utilized, or if in-stream uses were better recognized and protected. But as we have seen, the incentives for such changes do not exist under appropriationism. It was not developed with water quality issues in mind, and such issues cannot be easily addressed within its tenets.

Depletion through inefficiency and waste, discrimination against emergent uses and more qualitative values, and degradation of surface water quality—these are the major effects of appropriationism. As was argued in chapter 1, westerners can no longer afford to squander their available water resources, and it is quite apparent that noneconomic values have become and will continue to be important where water resources are concerned. But the extent and content of water rights under appropriationism make it very difficult, if not impossible, for these new concerns and values to be addressed. Given both the current state of western water and the region's interest in modifying future water use practices, the rigid structure of securing nearly absolute rights to the earliest users of water is no longer warranted.

Modifications to appropriationism have been made by state legislatures. By both expanding the notion of beneficial use and specifying preferred uses for times of shortage, the various western states have responded to some of the doctrine's shortcomings. Other statutes might mandate minimum quality standards or other regulations. However, there are those who insist that such developments are ill conceived; they believe that an open free market is the best determinant of the value of water. What is deemed more beneficial or preferred should, they believe, be a direct reflection of the price people are willing to pay for it: "Preferred use statutes are a mitigating factor, but even they are rigid in contrast to the flexibility and adaptability of the free market."[68] If a junior appropriator wants more security, let him buy water rights from a senior appropriator; if Los Angeles wants more security, let it buy out farmers; if people want places for recreation and scenic beauty, let them get together and purchase the water rights.

There are several problems with such arguments, as will be discussed more thoroughly in chapter 5. The sum of these problems, though, is that people have analogized from the case of other scarce resources to the case of water. Certainly the early proponents of appropriationism analogized from mining precious metals to utilizing water resources; and although many philosophers and economists have made the same sort of move, I argue that it is nevertheless the wrong one. We need to understand, in a more general way, what a property right is, how people legally or morally come to have them, and how such rights relate to the resource in question before the disanalogy between water and other resources becomes clear. It is to that task that I now turn.

NOTES

1. Donald J. Pisani, *Water, Land, and Law in the West* (Lawrence: University of Kansas Press, 1996), 9.

2. Harold Demsetz, "Toward a Theory of Property Rights," *American Economic Review, Papers, and Proceedings* 57 (1967): 347–359; see also Terry L. Anderson and P. J. Hill, "The Evolution of Property Rights: A Study of the American West," *Journal of Law and Economics* 18 (1975): 163–179.

3. See Frank J. Trelease, "The Model Water Code: The Wise Administrator and the Goddam Bureaucrat," *Natural Resources Journal* 14 (April 1974): 207–229.

4. William Goldfarb, *Water Law*, 2d ed. (Chelsea, MI: Lewis, 1988), 21.

5. Walter Prescott Webb, *The Great Plains* (Waltham, MA: Blaisdale, 1959), 433.

6. Goldfarb, *Water Law*, 22.

7. Donald Worster, *Rivers of Empire: Water, Aridity, and the Growth of the American West* (New York: Random House, Pantheon Books, 1985; reprint, New York: Oxford University Press, 1992), 88.

8. William Blackstone, *Commentaries on the Laws of England*, 11th ed., bk. 2 (London: Strahan and Woodfall, 1791), chapter 2, 18. Flowing water is thus classed with wild game and other so-called fugitive resources, meaning ones that must be captured before they can be used.

9. See Goldfarb, *Water Law*, 22; and Webb, *Great Plains*, 454.

10. *Merritt v. Parker*, quoted in Morton Horwitz, *The Transformation of American Law, 1780–1860* (Cambridge, MA: Harvard University Press, 1977), 35.

11. Horwitz, *Transformation of American Law*, 31.

12. Goldfarb, *Water Law*, 23.

13. Horwitz, *Transformation of American Law*, 30.

14. Quoted in Horwitz, *Transformation of American Law*, 37.

15. See Pisani, *Water, Land, and Law in the West*, 9.

16. Chancellor Kent, quoted in Horwitz, *Transformation of American Law*, 43.

17. *Cary v. Daniels*, 49 Mass. (8 Met) (1844), at 466–477.

18. Goldfarb, *Water Law*, 23.

19. Ibid., 39.

20. Ibid., 23.

21. *Cary v. Daniels*, at 477, emphasis added.

22. Horwitz, *Transformation of American Law*, 43; see also Pisani, *Water, Land, and Law in the West*, 9–10.

23. Goldfarb, *Water Law*, 23. There is considerable debate among historians about whether the early nineteenth-century water doctrine in the East is better characterized as prior appropriation or riparianism. Horwitz sees the nineteenth-century eastern courts' early acceptance and then ultimate rejection of prior appropriation as downright Machiavellian: "How better to develop an economy than initially to provide the first developers with guarantees against future competitive injury? And once development has reached a certain level, can the claims of still greater efficiency through competition be denied? By changing the rules and disguising the changes in the complexities of technical legal doctrine, the facade of economic security can be maintained even as new property is allowed to sweep away the old." See Horwitz, *Transformation of American Law*, 34.

24. David Hume, *A Treatise of Human Nature*, bk. 3, pt. 2, sec. 3, ed. L. A. Selby-Bigge (Oxford: Clarendon, 1888), 505–506.

25. Ibid., 509.

26. Ibid., 511n, emphasis added. In this footnote, which spans five pages, Hume discusses in great detail the origin and limitations of the assignment of property by accession. It is, he thinks, a process engendered by the natural propensity of our imagination, namely, its "agility" in connecting like ideas; it is, however, a fragile and "unsteady" process, because it is easily deflected. The contiguity of an unowned, small object to an owned, large object almost always leads to the imagination's association of that small object to the owner of the large object. The reverse association, however, is easily thwarted.

27. David Hume, "An Enquiry concerning the Principles of Morals, Appendix 3," in David Hume, *Enquiries concerning Human Understanding and concerning the Principles of Morals*, 3d ed., ed. L. A. Selby-Bigge (Oxford: Clarendon, 1975), 309.

28. Hume, *Treatise of Human Nature*, 514–515.

29. See Horwitz, *Transformation of American Law*, 34–35.

30. Goldfarb, *Water Law*, 35; see also Frank J. Trelease, "Uneasy Federalism—State Water Laws and National Water Uses," *Washington Law Review* 55 (November 1980): 752–753.

31. See Frank E. Maloney, *A Model Water Code: With Commentary* (Gainesville: University of Florida Press, 1972).

32. See Goldfarb, *Water Law*, 26–29.

33. See Alfred Z. Cuzán, "Appropriators versus Expropriators: The Political Economy of Water in the West," in *Water Rights: Scarce Resource Allocation, Bureaucracy, and the Environment*, ed. Terry L. Anderson (Cambridge, MA: Ballinger Publishing for the Pacific Institute for Public Policy Research, 1983), 19; Chennat Gopalakrishnan, "The Doctrine of Prior Appropriation and Its Impact on Water Development," *The American Journal of Economics and Sociology* 32 (1973): 61–65; and Pisani, *Water, Land, and Law in the West*, 22.

34. Worster, *Rivers of Empire*, 88.

35. As to what happens if two or more individuals appropriate simultaneously, the law is silent here. In practice, a system of permits has been implemented in most western states to facilitate the determination of priority (and, importantly, not to augment priority as the main consideration). If two permits are filed—and approved—simultaneously, then ancillary considerations might well come into play. However, I am not aware of any examples where the court or administrative agency did not arrive at a determination that one or the other claimant had priority and doled out water rights based on that priority. Western administrative permit systems are discussed later in this chapter.

36. Goldfarb, *Water Law*, 33.

37. Worster, *Rivers of Empire*, 90.

38. The Mormons settled in the West in 1847, and began their irrigation practices before the miners came to California. They were a closed and closely-knit community, and they developed their own water laws independent of the broader development in the region. Because the Mormons'

laws were rejected elsewhere and, ultimately, replaced by prior appropriation, the Mormon experience is generally given only anecdotal treatment by historians of western water law. For more information, see Worster, *Rivers of Empire*, 74–83; and Pisani, *Water, Land, and Law in the West*, 16–17.

39. Pisani, *Water, Land, and Law in the West*, 24.

40. It was not until 1860 that Congress began to enact legislation officially recognizing miners' claims to land in the public domain. Until then, state and territorial courts were the primary vehicles for shaping the law. See Pisani, *Water, Land, and Law in the West*, 12–15.

41. Pisani, *Water, Land, and Law in the West*, 10–11.

42. Strictly speaking, this is incorrect. The Spanish and Mexicans had established their own doctrines for water in the region. The Anglo settlers ignored these, as well as the older "pueblo" doctrines; prior appropriation developed virtually independent of all these. See Webb, *Great Plains*, 439–442; and Pisani, *Water, Land, and Law in the West*, 18.

43. This distinction is lost on many property theorists, who talk as if certain resources just *are* common property. As Daniel W. Bromley writes, "There is no such thing as a common property *resource*; there are only resources controlled and managed as common property, or as state property, or as private property." See Daniel W. Bromley, *Environment and Economy: Property Rights and Public Policy* (Oxford: Basil Blackwell, 1991), 4. I return to this topic in chapters 3 and 5.

44. Pisani, *Water, Land, and Law in the West*, 11.

45. Ibid., 12; and Worster, *Rivers of Empire*, 89.

46. Cuzán, "Appropriators versus Expropriators," 18.

47. The term "senior appropriator" refers to order of temporal priority, not to location; it is possible to be either an upstream or downstream senior.

48. Pisani, *Water, Land, and Law in the West*, 23.

49. See Cuzán, "Appropriators versus Expropriators," 18–19; Goldfarb, *Water Law*, 33; Gopalakrishnan, "Doctrine of Prior Appropriation," 62; and Pisani, *Water, Land, and Law in the West*, 12.

50. See Pisani, *Water, Land, and Law in the West*, 12–13, 21; and Worster, *Rivers of Empire*, 90n, 136–137.

51. Gopalakrishnan, "Doctrine of Prior Appropriation," 65; see also Goldfarb, *Water Law*, 37.

52. See Goldfarb, *Water Law*, 30. Interbasin transfers have not occurred in the eastern United States largely because there has been no need to do so.

53. See Philip L. Fradkin, *A River No More: The Colorado River and the West* (Tucson: University of Arizona Press, 1981), 43.

54. Goldfarb, *Water Law*, 33–34.

55. Ibid., 34.

56. Ibid.

57. Worster, *Rivers of Empire*, 92.

58. Horwitz, *Transformation of American Law*, 34.

59. See Pisani, *Water, Land, and Law in the West*, 14–15.

60. Flood irrigation is one of the oldest and simplest forms of irrigating crops. Basically, water is applied at the high end of a field and flows down towards the low end. Drip irrigation is a more recent and highly efficient technique, largely pioneered and practiced by the Israelis. It is a technique that delivers water through a network of porous or perforated piping directly to the crops' roots. See Sandra Postel, "Water Scarcity," *Environmental Science and Technology* 26 (1992), 2332–2333.

61. See Goldfarb, *Water Law*, 35–36.

62. The intuitions of libertarians are similarly touched. Although Robert Nozick thinks that "particular rights over particular things fill the space of rights" and cannot, he thinks, be legitimately overridden, even he accepts and "feels the power" of intuitions to the contrary. See Robert Nozick, *Anarchy, State, and Utopia* (New York: Basic, 1974), 236–237; see also Will Kymlicka, *Contemporary Political Thought: An Introduction* (Oxford: Oxford University Press, 1990), 100–101.

63. *State ex rel. Cary et al. v. Cochran*, 292 N.W. (1940), at 239. Nebraska recognizes both the riparian and prior appropriation doctrines: the former is the rule of law in the wetter, eastern part of the state, and the latter in the drier, western part. In this case, however, prior appropriation was the only doctrine applicable.

64. Cochran, at 75.

65. See *Empire Water and Power Co. v. Cascade Town Co.*, 205 F. 123, 129 (1913); and *Idaho v. Coeur d'alene Tribe of Idaho*, 117 S. Ct. 2028, 2043 (1997).

66. See Goldfarb, *Water Law*, 35.

67. Ibid., 37, emphasis added.

68. Ibid., 41; see also Terry L. Anderson, ed., *Water Rights: Scarce Resource Allocation, Bureaucracy, and the Environment* (Cambridge, MA: Ballinger Publishing for the Pacific Institute for Public Policy Research, 1983); and Terry L. Anderson and Donald R. Leal, *Free Market Environmentalism* (San Francisco: Westview Press for the Pacific Institute for Public Policy, 1991).

3

The Structure of Property Rights and the Nature of Resources

> The central core of the notion of a property right in X, relative to which other parts of the notion are to be explained, is the right to determine what shall be done with X; the right to choose which of the constrained set of options concerning X shall be realized or attempted.
>
> Robert Nozick, *Anarchy, State, and Utopia*

INTRODUCTION

Contemporary philosophical discussions of property and ownership have, for the most part, been couched within a single conceptual framework. That framework, consisting of Wesley Newcomb Hohfeld's analysis of rights conjoined with A. M. Honoré's analysis of ownership, constitutes a perspicacious and versatile analytic tool. Not only does it allow us to describe adequately the various rights-relationships between persons and with respect to things that we find in our own culture, but it is also sufficient for describing all the forms of property or ownership we might encounter, "from tribal life through feudal society to modern industrial states."[1] The salient features of this framework are outlined in this chapter.

Despite the range of its applicability, the Hohfeld-Honoré framework has most often and extensively been used to analyze the structure of only one form of ownership: private ownership, or private property. The focus on private ownership is understandable, but nonetheless regrettable. It is understandable because, since at least the seventeenth century, private ownership has been the proverbial firebrand about which some of the most heated political and philosophical debates have raged. Its proponents have endlessly expounded the virtues of private ownership, and its critics have no less exhaustively cataloged its drawbacks. But the lack of an adequate conceptual framework, until quite recently, has meant that many of the earlier debates consisted in the disputants simply talking past one another. By grounding the discussion in mutually acceptable terms, contemporary proponents and critics of private property have made much progress in sorting out exactly what is at issue in such debates. Other than at either end of what John Chapman has called the "egalitarian teleocratic gradient," marked at one end by thoroughgoing libertarians and at the other end by absolute egalitarians, the disputants more or less agree that, at some times and for some things, private property is preferable; at other times and for other things, it is not.[2]

But some of the possible alternatives to private ownership have, regrettably, not been as fully elaborated as they need to be, and failure to adequately articulate the structure of such alternative rights-relationships has served to weaken arguments for their viability. Many critics of private-property regimes have themselves been roundly chastised for not having much to say about how the resources in question ought to be produced or distributed, except that market mechanisms are ruled out. In order to be taken seriously, the critic of private property must do more; she must, as N. Scott Arnold puts it, "specify alternative institutional arrangements and explain how the arrangements will solve or ameliorate the problem to which she has called attention."[3]

In this chapter, I am most centrally concerned with specifying one alternative to private ownership, what I call common-property arrangement. In such an arrangement, a limited group of individuals has property rights over a particular resource; ownership is in some sense vested in the group or resource community, which thus acquires the power to exclude nonmembers and to determine what shall be done with the resource by its individual members.[4] The structure of the rights-relationship between the resource community and its individual members will also be discussed.

Along with the neglect and misunderstanding of alternatives to private ownership, differences between *resources* have been inadequately treated in the philosophical literature. In addition, then, to understanding the structure of the rights-relationship in a common-property arrangement in terms of the Hohfeld-Honoré framework, we need to understand the nature of the resources for which such arrangements may be well suited. As Honoré himself says, "the notions of ownership and the thing owned are interdependent,"[5] suggesting that different resources are amenable to different forms of ownership. Later in this chapter, I offer a conceptual framework for analyzing the suitability of resources to common-property arrangements. By employing several notions culled from economics—jointness, excludability, and indivisibility—we can identify a subset of resources for which a common-property arrangement *may be* a viable form of ownership. For those resources, it must then be shown that a common-property arrangement is in fact preferable to private property. Such matters are addressed more directly in the final three chapters.

My position, then, is that sometimes private property, or private ownership, is the best way to utilize scarce resources; sometimes, however, a common-property arrangement promises better utilization of such resources. This claim constitutes neither an unmitigated attack on the concept of private property, nor a wholesale endorsement of common-property arrangements; rather, it represents an argument in favor of social institutions that are well adapted to particular resources. Before the case can be made that a common-property arrangement is, in fact, better suited to water in the West than is private ownership, we first need to have a general idea of what a common-property arrangement looks like and what sorts of resources are possible candidates for such an arrangement.

THE STRUCTURE OF PROPERTY RIGHTS

As Lawrence C. Becker writes, "Property rights . . . are the rights of ownership. In every case, to have a property right in a thing is to have a bundle of rights that defines a form of ownership."[6] That is, we know what form of ownership exists in a particular situation when we have determined the nature and distribution of the existing property rights. Before we can carry out this determination, we first need to understand what property rights are and how they relate to other sorts of rights. Accordingly, I discuss the various notions of a "right," and then the concept of property rights, or the rights of ownership.

The Concept of a "Right"

In the most general sense, a "right" is a moral or legal relationship between persons that is advantageous to, or beneficial for, the person who has or possesses the right. But the variable nature of such relationships has engendered a vocabulary that acknowledges at least four sorts of advantages, or benefits, associated with the term "right." The source for this vocabulary is Hohfeld, a legal theorist, though the actual terminology used here is borrowed from Becker.[7]

The first sort of right—and what Hohfeld maintains is, in the strictest sense, the only kind of right—is a *claim-right*.[8] The existence of a claim-right for one person entails the existence of a *duty* for another. If, for example, I have a claim-right to $100 from you, then you have a moral or legal duty to pay it to me. If you fail to pay me the $100, then, other things being equal, it would be justifiable to (try to) extract the payment from you or to (try to) get from you some other type of compensation or satisfaction: maybe you have to mow my lawn for a week or must go to jail for a month. We could further distinguish the claim-rights held by groups of people against either individuals or other groups of people, but the basic idea would be the same. If a person or persons have a claim-right, then some other person or persons have a duty to either perform or forebear from performing some action.

The second type of right identified by Hohfeld is a *liberty*.[9] A liberty can be understood as a permission: If I have a liberty to do or forebear from doing some thing, then I am permitted to either do or not do the thing, and no one else has a moral or legal claim-right against me to either act or forebear. For example, I have the liberty of giving $100 to a charity, but I have no duty to do so, and the charity has no claim-right to my $100 if I fail to give it to them. Similarly, my right to score a goal in a soccer game does not entail that the other team has a duty to let me score: *they* are at liberty to stop *me*. Whereas claim-rights entail duties, liberties entail the absence of claim-rights and, therefore, the absence of duties; liberties, we could say, entail no-rights.

Different from both claim-rights and liberties are *powers*, the third sort of right Hohfeld identifies. A person has a power, or a power-right, when, by some act, he or she can change his or her rights-relationship or that of someone else. My right to make a will, for example, is a power I have to alter my relations to others with respect to their rights. As Becker puts it, "The existence of a power right is the existence of a state of affairs such that one person (the right-holder) may morally (or legally) alter at will some of the rights, duties, liberties, powers or immunities of another person (the liability-bearer)."[10] The existence of a power in one person entails a *liability* in another. If I have the power of leaving you an expensive watch in my will, then you have the liability of having your rights altered vis-à-vis that watch. This example highlights the fact that liabilities need not be disadvantageous. Rather, a liability should be understood merely as a susceptibility to having one's moral or legal rights altered by someone else. Still, such susceptibility is generally disadvantageous. If nothing else, liability-bearers live with perpetual uncertainty regarding the security of their various rights.

Finally, there are *immunities*, which can be understood simply as a lack of susceptibility to having one's rights altered. If I cannot compel you to sell your watch, then you have an immunity against me; I have no power to alter your rights vis-à-vis the watch. Similarly, in our society, people are immune from being married without their consent; no one has the power to force people into marrying one another. A lack of such powers can be considered a *disability*, and the existence of an immunity in one person entails a disability in another.

So, claim-rights, liberties, powers, and immunities can all be considered rights, or right-surrogates. Their unifying feature is that they are all benefits secured to individuals by promulgated and generally accepted rules, be they moral rules or parts of a codified legal system. This can be seen more clearly if we consider that their respective opposites—duties, no-rights, liabilities, and disabilities—all generally connote disadvantages to those who are so constrained. That, after all, is why we tend to want more of the former sort of things and fewer of the latter sort.

I have characterized "rights" in rather broad terms, and a brief comment is in order about the difference between *legal* rights and *moral* rights. Whereas a *legal* claim-right carries with it the expectation that, should the duty-bearer not perform his duty, it would be justifiable to use legally sanctioned remedies (fines, imprisonment, and so on) to extract something from him, a claim-right considered as a *moral* right need not carry with it any such expectations. Rather, if I have a moral expectation about your performance or forbearance of an act, although your failure to act as expected might result in some legally sanctioned reaction, it might well result only in expressions of contempt, severance of cordial relations, or other forms of social ostracism.[11] That is, the existence of legal mechanisms is not necessary for the existence of claim-rights, and other sorts of rights, per se. What does seem minimally necessary, though not sufficient, for both legal and moral rights is this: They are considered by the group to which they apply to be standards or conventions "to which [people] attribute a certain type of value and which, by virtue of this belief, they treat as a valid norm governing their actions."[12] Moreover, when deviations from such norms occur, there is a high probability that such deviations "will result in a relatively general and practically significant reaction of disapproval."[13] More generally, then, whenever a person expects that because of the existence of mutually understood norms his or her performance or forbearance of an act will result in significant reactions of disapproval, then rights of some sort can be said to exist. This subject is discussed further in the next chapter and again in chapter 6; it is raised here only to highlight the fact that the existence of claim-rights and other sorts of rights need not depend on the existence of a codified and promulgated legal system.[14]

The Rights of Ownership

By combining a Hohfeldian analysis of rights and their opposites with an analysis of the elements of ownership offered by Honoré, we can get an adequate understanding of the general concept of ownership, or property. Honoré identifies eleven elements, or "incidents" as he calls them, that, when taken together, are supposed to constitute "the greatest possible interest in a thing which a mature system of law recognizes."[15] These Honoréan elements are: the rights to possess, use, and manage a thing; the right to the income from a thing; the right to the capital of a thing; the duty to prevent harmful use of a thing; the right to transmit a thing; the liability to execution; the right to security; the absence of term; and residuary rules. Each of these elements will be considered in turn, although some require only a passing comment. Also, the number eleven is not sacrosanct. Honoré allows that it is possible to combine or split out some of the elements into others, and as we shall see, recombining and splitting out some of the elements allows us to make more fine-grained distinctions with regard to property rights.

The first Honoréan element of ownership is the right to possess a thing; it is the right to have exclusive physical control of some object, and it constitutes "the foundation on which the whole superstructure of ownership rests."[16] If I have the right to possess a particular desk, for example, what I have is not merely a *power* to take possession of it, nor is it simply a *liberty* to keep possession of it. Rather, it is a (moral or legal) *claim-right* that my physical control over the desk be protected both now and in the future. If I have the right to possess

a particular desk, others have a duty not to interfere with my possession of it, and perhaps even a duty to see to it that the desk is restored
to me if it is lost or stolen.[17]

The right to use the desk, that is, to personally enjoy the benefits of
it, is part *claim-right* and part *liberty*. From what was said earlier, if
all I have is the liberty of using the desk, then others have no duty to
refrain from at least attempting to use it as well. And if others have
an equal liberty of using it or of attempting to use it, which is what a
lack of duty on their part suggests, then it would be wrong to say that
my mere use of the desk alone constitutes either a property right in
or a form of ownership of the desk. That is why Becker stipulates
that the right to use a thing is primarily a liberty, but in order to be a
property right, it must be "reinforced with claim rights excluding
others from interference."[18] It is only when my liberty of using the
desk is reinforced by a claim-right that others refrain from attempting to use it that the right rises to the level of a property right.[19]

The right to manage a desk, that is, to decide how and by whom the
desk shall be used, is a conglomeration of liberties and powers reinforced by exclusive claim-rights. The right to manage a thing is, as
Robert Nozick suggests in the opening quote to this chapter, one of
the primary elements of ownership: "The central core of the notion of
a property right in X, relative to which other parts of the notion are to
be explained, is the right to determine what shall be done with X; the
right to choose which of the constrained set of options concerning X
shall be realized or attempted."[20] This is echoed by Honoré, who
writes that sometimes:

> The complex of powers which make up the right to manage is . . .
> most prominent. The power to direct how resources are to be
> used and exploited is one of the cardinal types of economic and
> political power. . . . Many observers have drawn attention to the
> growth of managerial power divorced from legal ownership. *In
> such cases it may be that we should speak of split ownership or
> redefine our notion of the thing owned.*[21]

In common-property arrangements, the right to manage a thing is
divorced or split off from other elements of ownership. And as will be
discussed, we indeed get a clearer understanding of common-property arrangements by redefining our notion of what is owned in such
a state of affairs.

The fourth Honoréan element of ownership, the right to income, is
straightforwardly a claim-right, and it may be thought of as a surro-

gate of the right to use some thing. If I forego personally using my desk, then I may nevertheless be said to "enjoy" it by deriving income from someone else's temporary use of it. So, the right to use a thing can either be split out to distinguish various connotations of use, and thereby pick out separable rights of ownership, or it can be thought of as referring to use broadly and generally. If we consider the fifth Honoréan element, the right to the capital of a thing, we can see that it, too, can be split out into separate elements: the right to wholly consume or destroy the thing; the right to modify it in some way less than wholly consuming or destroying it; and the right to alienate it by sale, gift, or abandonment.[22] Splitting out the right to the capital of a thing in this way highlights the fact that one who has this right has both the *liberty* to destroy or modify the thing as well as the *power* to alienate it. Also, by distinguishing the separable rights to either destroy or modify my desk, we can see that such rights are liberties to *use* or use *up* the desk, and, therefore, that the right to the capital of a thing can be considered as a more specific instance of a general right to use it. The right to income from and the right to capital of a thing are discussed more fully in the next chapter.

With regard to the sixth Honoréan element, the duty to prevent harmful use, some theorists maintain that such duties or prohibitions are, as Jeremy Waldron puts it, "better regarded as general background constraints on action than as specific rules of property."[23] While I generally agree with Waldron, "harmful use" has a broad range of connotations. The prohibition against dropping my desk on your head or sticking my knife into your chest should not be seen as a property rule per se, but rather as a background condition, one established by other principles or laws operating in society.[24] But if I use my knife to whittle a better whistle than you and thereby attract your whistle customers to my product, there is a clear sense in which my right to use my knife has harmed you. Be that as it may, here I will follow Waldron in not treating the duty to prevent harm as an element of ownership. Later, in chapter 5, harmful use will be discussed again under the guise of negative externalities.

Neither of the next two Honoréan elements, the right to transmit a thing and the liability to execution, do not require much discussion. The former can be understood simply as the power to bequeath some thing to someone else; the latter as the liability of having the thing taken away under certain circumstances (e.g., as compensation for an unpaid debt).[25]

Honoré's ninth element, the right to security, is simply an immunity from expropriation, as is the next element, the absence of term.

They both, as Becker puts it, "correlate with disabilities in others."[26] However, they can both be further understood by considering the last Honoréan element of ownership, residuary rules. Such rules govern the reversion to another, if any, of ownership rights that have expired. They include, for instance, the rule for determining the reversion of rights upon the expiration of a lease.[27] If, for example, I have the rights of possession, use, and management of a desk for an indeterminate length of time, then there is an absence of term on such rights, and my immunity from expropriation holds indefinitely. There is no one to whom such rights revert, and because of this— cases of split ownership aside—I would normally be called the owner of the desk. But if such rights are for a determinate length of time, then I am liable to expropriation when that time expires. And the person to whom such rights revert would normally be called the owner of the desk. I say normally because the person to whom my rights revert might in turn have his or her rights revert to someone else: for example, I may have sublet an apartment from you, which you, in turn, have rented from someone else. So I might well expect immunity from expropriation for the term of my lease, but such immunity does not entail an absence of term. However, an absence of term does entail immunity from expropriation.

So, with regard to some "ownable" thing, if all of the Honoréan elements were determined to inhere in one individual in a particular situation, then that individual would have all of the elements or rights of ownership that a mature system of law recognizes, and we would no doubt say that the thing was that individual's private property. Where only some of the elements are applicable or where the applicable elements are split among several individuals, characterizing the form of ownership so constituted becomes less straightforward. The Honoréan elements of ownership with which I am most centrally concerned going forward are the rights of possession, use, and management, where use is conceived of broadly enough to include personally enjoying the thing, deriving income from it by selling it or leasing it to someone else, and modifying or using the thing up entirely. While use and possession seem quite intimately connected, management seems more able to stand alone. As we shall see, it is when the rights of use and possession are split off from the rights of management that we are dealing, potentially, with a common-property arrangement.

FORMS OF OWNERSHIP

Although the inherence in one individual of all the elements of ownership discussed in the previous section would constitute ownership in the fullest sense possible, we rarely if ever encounter such a state of affairs. As with many other concepts in philosophy, full exclusive ownership is best understood as an "ideal type" against which other, actual states of affairs can be compared. It is a heuristic device, useful for organizing our ideas about the forms of property or the character of property-rights arrangements that we might either encounter or propose. As such, "The organizing idea of a private property system is that, in principle, *each resource belongs to some individual . . . whose determination as to the use of the resource is taken as final.*"[28] This suggests that when a particular resource does not, in principle, belong to some individual, or when an individual's determination vis-à-vis that resource is, in fact, subject to emendation by others, then we are dealing with something other than private property. After first characterizing private property and then briefly discussing two other forms of ownership in terms of such determination, the discussion then turns to the main task of this section: characterizing common-property arrangements in similar terms.

With regard to property, the term "individual" can apply to entities other than "natural" persons. Such entities include partnerships, corporations, and other legally bound conglomerations of individuals. Both Stephen P. Munzer and Waldron consider partnerships, corporations, and so on as "artificial" persons, and they discuss corporate ownership as a type, or mutation, of private ownership.[29] I follow them here. I take it that such entities make decisions vis-à-vis some ownable object that more or less equate to determinations made by a single individual; each such entity operates as a single decision-making unit, at least as far as those decision-making units other than that entity itself are concerned. As such, partnerships, corporations, and the like should be considered as artificial persons or individuals.

Private Property

The inherence in one individual of the entire collection of Honoréan elements specifies jointly sufficient conditions for full, exclusive ownership. Yet we typically and easily recognize ownership in cases where only a limited subset of such elements inheres in a particular individual: for example, a trust fund is no doubt mine even though I might lack certain rights over it. More generally, there "are not individually necessary conditions for the person of inherence to be designated the owner of a particular thing."[30] That is, no one Honoréan element needs to be present in order for private ownership, or private property, to be recognized. Lack of precision in specifying necessary and sufficient conditions for private property has led one commentator, Thomas C. Grey, to insist that private property "ceases to be an important category in legal and political theory."[31] However, most other commentators nevertheless conclude that, despite our inability to nail down a watertight analytic definition, the term "private property" is useful and important for political and social theory.[32] In some marginal cases, it might not matter too much whether we label a relationship "private ownership" or something else, but there are enough clear-cut cases to render the distinction apropos.

Starting from the ideal case of full, exclusive ownership, which elements can be eliminated and yet the idea remain alive that some one individual's determination as to the use of the resource is taken as final? At this point, we are not considering potential cases of split ownership, where the absent elements inhere in someone else. Nor are we concerned with situations where residuary rules might come into play. Rather, we are first concerned with states of affairs where some Honoréan elements simply do not apply.

With regard to a desk, if an individual, Eve, had all the elements of ownership save the power to transmit, or bequeath, it, then it would still make sense to say that Eve owned the desk. While alive, she and she alone would still be able to control how and by whom the desk was used, and she could reap the other advantages of either using or foregoing use of it. She could modify, destroy, or sell the desk, or she could simply let it sit unused in the corner of her house. The indeterminate length of her life means that there is an indeterminate duration on her control of all such activities. Another way to think of this is that if Eve initially had the power to transmit the desk, but was subsequently denied this power, then none of the other advantages she had would be affected very much. While there is still an "Eve" around, her determinations as to the use of the desk would still be final. It is not even the case that her options vis-à-vis such determinations are minimally constrained: Her power to transmit the desk, if she had it, would perhaps make the desk more valuable, but even without that power, her rights to the income from and capital of the desk are still quite expansive.[33]

Suppose that what Eve possessed was not a desk, but was instead some other object, one beyond her or anyone's power to change it, such as a meteor impervious to any of our attempts to modify it. In this case, Eve's actual ability to determine the fate of the object is constrained, but so is everyone else's. The set of options concerning what shall be realized or attempted with the meteor is limited, but not by any feature of human law or morality. Within these physical constraints on everyone, and in addition to Eve's lack of power to transmit the meteor to her children, it still seems clear that she owns the meteor. She can still *use* it, for example, to hold down a stack of paper, or she can give, lease, or sell it to someone else; she can even charge and collect admission for others to view it. So the power to modify or destroy the thing appears to be eliminable from the concept of private property. More generally, the idea that using some thing *requires* materially transforming or consuming it seems obviously false.

Starting from the other end and asking what minimal rights need to be present in order for someone to be accorded ownership of some thing, we can see that if possession, use, or management is secured indefinitely to an individual, then we have a form of private ownership. If someone presently had any of these three elements, and if that element was secured or buttressed with a claim-right against expropriation for an indeterminate length of time, that is, there is an absence of term, then that individual could support his or her claim of being *the* owner. Again, we are not considering cases where these elements are split among various parties, for example, where one person has (secure) use rights and another has (secure) rights of management. Rather, we are only considering cases where one or some of these elements do, and will continue to, inhere in one person.

This almost makes it sound as if the right to security could stand alone as a form of private ownership. But as Becker points out, this right is "parasitic on other elements: Immunity from expropriation of what *right?* is always a question that must be answered in applying this element."[34] So, too, are the elements of the absence of term, liability to execution, and residuary rules parasitic on other elements: *What* rights are immune from expropriation, liable to be taken away, or will revert to someone else?

The right to the capital of a thing seems as though it could also be a stand-alone indicator of private ownership. Becker initially thought so: "The right to the capital is the only one of the elements which seems able to define a variety of ownership standing alone . . . if only because it includes the right to destroy, consume, and alienate."[35] Later on, he not only split out this element into three separate ones, but he also added that any of the three could stand as a variety of private ownership only when "it is supplemented by some version of the right to security."[36] And this sounds more correct.

The discussion here, though brief, has, hopefully, brought out the salient features of private property, or private ownership. An individual need not have the powers to bequeath, modify, or destroy something in order to own it. What an individual does need, though, is some measure of long-term security in one or several of the Honoréan rights of possession, use, or management vis-à-vis some ownable thing. If an individual has such rights, and where no one else can claim any of those rights that that individual lacks, then that person, and that person alone, can determine what shall be done with the thing. In short, private property is marked by a state of affairs where there is one entity "whose determination as to the use of the resource is taken as final."[37] Such entities are primarily individuals, although they could be partnerships, corporations, or other legally bound or artificial persons.

What Common-Property Arrangements Are Not

Before giving a positive account of common-property arrangements in terms of the relevant Honoréan elements, a few words are in order concerning some prevalent misconceptions about such states of affairs. These misconceptions are mentioned here both to support my previous cryptic remarks about the neglect and misunderstanding of common-property arrangements, and to mark the boundaries of the Scylla and Charybdis, as it were, that such misunderstandings have engendered for common-property advocates. These matters are discussed further in chapter 5.

Waldron devotes one page of an almost five-hundred-page book on property to discussing common property. He states: "Many philosophers have used the idea of common property to characterize the initial situation of men in relation to resources in the so-called 'state of Nature.' "[38] That he himself is one of the many becomes quite clear when, in a brief and tangential comment a few pages later, he characterizes common property thus: "people simply make use of [resources] as they want to."[39] Many economists have a similar view. Douglas North and Robert P. Thomas, for instance, write that in primitive societies, "natural resources, whether the animals to be hunted or vegetation to be gathered, were initially held as common property. This type of property right implies free access by all to the resource."[40]

Such characterizations, however, describe *no* form of property; rather, they merely describe a state of affairs where everyone has *liberties* that are unsupported by moral or legal claim-rights, powers, or immunities of any sort. If we recall my initial characterization of a common-property arrangement—a situation where a limited set of individuals has use rights, but ownership is in some sense vested in the group, which thus acquires the power to determine what shall be done with the resource by its individual members—we see that not only does it include claim-rights and powers, but also that such rights are limited to a specific group of people. So, common-property arrangements should not be construed as so-called negative communities, where the resource is owned by no one but equally available to everyone.[41]

Nor are advocates of common-property arrangements simply arguing for a variant of state property, as some commentators seem to think. With even less attention than Waldron gives it, Munzer writes, "Contrasted with private property are various sorts of *public property*. Here the owners are the state, city, community or tribe."[42] The common feature of public-property arrangements is that final determinations as to the use of a resource are, to a significant degree, vested in some sovereign authority: The resource "belongs to" the sovereign authority, and how and by whom the resource is used is dictated by the government or its agencies rather than by individuals or private organizations. Common-property arrangements share one feature of such public-property arrangements: In both, individuals are no longer free to determine for themselves how to use the resource. But a common-property arrangement differs from public property in this respect: "[Individuals] participate in a process of collective choice that sets limits on individual use."[43] In other words, the decision-making arrangements in a common-property arrangement are such that *who* makes the decisions and for *whom* such decisions are made are one and the same group of people. This differs quite markedly from the sorts of public-property arrangements Munzer has in mind, where the decision makers are typically courts, legislatures, officials, or agencies that are readily distinguishable, functionally, from those for whom the decisions are made.

Common-Property Arrangements

A common-property arrangement is also known as common ownership, common property, or a common-property relationship. However, I use "common-property arrangement," both to minimize possible confusion and to highlight the various ways in which ownership can be understood. Since Waldron maintains that " 'ownership' is a term peculiar to systems of private property,"[44] it seems best to avoid the first label. I term it an "arrangement" rather than a "relationship" because the latter term primarily connotes connections among persons. But "property" also connotes connections between persons and things. Since I am concerned with both connotations, "arrangement" is chosen as a more neutral and encompassing descriptor.

The relevant entities in a common-property arrangement are the group or resource community as a whole and its individual members. The individual members could be considered either individual or artificial persons. Determining group, or community, membership is an important issue, one that is intimately connected to the physical and technical attributes of the resource in question. Such matters are discussed in the next section, and again in chapter 6. However, it should be noted here that membership need not be limited to *direct* users of the resource. Since effects of resource use can cross from one resource to another (e.g., my water use may affect another's land use), those *materially affected* by direct uses of a resource might have to be included in the resource community as well. In addition, we are concerned with instances of resource scarcity, where not everyone who wants to use the resource directly can do so without thereby interfering with others' uses. This means that even if membership is limited to those who can use the resource directly, either not all members can be using it at any one time, or not all members can be using it to the extent they would like.

The preceding remarks suggest that the initial characterization of a common-property arrangement as a state of affairs where a limited set of individuals has use rights is in need of some refinement. Since not all members of the resource community need to be (direct) users of the resource, rights to use the resource need not extend to all of its members. And since not all those to whom such rights *do* extend can either use the resource simultaneously or use it simultaneously to the extent they would like, the (direct) users must have *limited* use rights. Adding to this the observation that the members of the resource community participate in a process of collective choice that sets limits on individuals' uses, a more refined characterization of a common-property arrangement is this: It is a state of affairs where (only) the members of the resource community have *limited* rights to use the resource, and where such limits are determined by a process of collective choice in which the members of the resource community are responsible for such determinations. In such an arrangement, the members' rights are determined by the members themselves, each on a coequal footing. (This characterization has led some theorists to suggest that a common-property arrangement could be considered a *form* of private property: private property *for the group of co-owners*.[45] It is a suggestion worth noting, but not one pursued further here.)

The previous characterization does, however, raise several other questions. Some have to do with the process itself: Must all members *directly* participate in the process? Can they participate through representatives? How are decisions reached? Must there be unanimous, two-thirds agreement, or a simple majority? And how are the resource community's decisions enforced? A discussion of these sorts of questions is left to chapter 6. Here, the focus is on other sorts of questions, specifically those having to do with the rights about which the process is concerned: Which rights belong to the resource community, and which belong to its members? What is the nature of these rights? And how should we characterize the rights-relationship between these two entities?

In a common-property arrangement, ownership, as Ronald J. Oakerson puts it, "is *in some sense* vested in the group, which thus acquires the power to regulate the commons and to exclude others."[46] The power to regulate is the power to determine how and by whom the resource can be used. Earlier, this power was identified as the right, or power-right, to manage the resource. Oakerson is saying, then, that because the resource community in some sense owns the resource, the community therefore has this power. Conversely, because *individual* members of the resource community lack the power to regulate how and by whom the resource can be used, they lack managerial power, and there is some sense, then, in which they are *not* the owners. This implies that there is at least *a* sense in which the members *do* own the resource. Also, if an individual owns something, he or she must have relatively secure rights to possess, manage, or use it, where use may include any or all of: the right of personal use, the right to the income, or the rights to the capital of the thing. Since managerial power is out, the sense in which individual members own the resource must issue from the fact that they have claim-rights to either possess or use it. Although the determination of these rights is largely beyond the control of any individual member of the resource community, it is to individual members that such rights are extended, and it is for them that such rights exist. It is the individual members of the resource community who possess and use the resource, and not the resource community considered in itself. Even so, in virtue of managerial power possessed by the resource community, it seems more correct to say that the resource community is *the* owner.

It is when the elements of ownership are split between two or more entities that the "in some sense" qualification has force. In a common-property arrangement, the resource community has the right of management, and individual members have at least some of the rights of possession and use. This state of affairs represents managerial power largely divorced from the other elements of ownership. It is in just such a state of affairs that Honoré suggests, "it may be that we should speak of split ownership or redefine our notion of the thing owned."[47] Simply settling on labeling it "split ownership," however, fails to clear up some important matters. Redefining our notion of the thing owned, however, does clear them up.

Speaking of split ownership presents us with difficulties. Often it is the case that we want to establish who is the owner of some thing as a first step toward settling other issues. For example, only the owner of a desk can sell it, and if two people are trying to sell it, establishing who is *the* owner is a necessary first step for determining who has the right to sell it. If, however, all we can say is that ownership is split, and that there is not *one* owner, then that determination alone will not help us. When Waldron discusses split ownership, he essentially attempts to analyze it away. He suggests that where ownership is in dispute because use rights are split off from other elements of ownership, we can always look to residuary rules and use them to settle matters definitively one way or the other: "We have to examine something of the history of the uses and rights. . . . We must examine not just the way that resources are being used at this minute but how it was determined that *that* use . . . came about."[48] All else being equal, Adam's current use of the desk implies that he is the owner. But if Eve leased him the desk, *that* implies that Eve really owns it. By viewing the matter diachronically, we can establish Eve as the real owner, and it is not then really a case of split ownership. At some point in the future the desk will again be possessed by Eve; it will belong to her. If it can be sold, then she is the only one who has the power to do so. But we said earlier that in common-property arrangements, in terms of possessing and using a resource, the resource does *not*, in a significant sense, belong to the resource community. The resource community does not itself use the resource; rather, it uses its rights of management to determine which of its members may use it.

What I am suggesting is that in common-property arrangements we get a clearer picture of what is going on, and a fuller understanding of the sense in which the resource community is *the* owner, if we say that what the resource community has or owns are the *rights of ownership*; that is, what belongs to the resource community are certain *rights* to determine the rights of its individual members. This might seem to obfuscate matters more than it clears anything up, but under closer inspection such apparent obscurity becomes more intelligible.

In a section of his paper entitled "The Thing Owned," Honoré argues against such a move. He considers whether "the thing owned should always be spoken of as a right. This is an odd-looking proposal, since owning involves having certain rights in a thing. If, therefore, we are to substitute for 'owning a pen' 'owning certain rights in a pen,' it would seem to follow that the owner should correctly be said to have certain rights in certain rights in a pen.... But why stop at the second order of rights?"[49] There are, however, two reasons for not going along with Honoré here. First, I am not proposing that the thing owned should always (or only) be spoken of as a right. Rather, what I *am* proposing is that in just the sort of situation Honoré himself finds puzzling—where managerial power is largely divorced from the other elements of ownership—we can better understand what is going on by focusing on the rights-relationship between the entity with managerial powers and the entities that actually possess and use the resource. By doing so, we can see the sense in which ownership can be attributed to the resource community in virtue of its rights over its members' rights.

Second, Honoré's example is not a case of potential split ownership; the pen clearly belongs to one person; it is Eve's exclusively. His skepticism about characterizing Eve's relationship to the pen wholly in terms of rights is directed at the possibility of infinite regress. I take it that his worry is this: Although we *could* say that Eve's ownership of the pen is wholly constituted by the fact that she has certain rights to use it, this would imply that we could also say that "she has the right to use the right to use the pen." And if we can do *this*, then what principled reason do we have for stopping there, since by iterative substitution we could go on to a tertiary order of use rights, and so on? But in common-property arrangements there are *two different entities* involved, and the "certain rights" belonging to one entity are different than those belonging to the other. There *is* a principled reason for saying that "the resource community has the right to manage its members' right to use the resource": It helps us to better understand the nature of the relationship between the resource community and its members in terms of Hohfeldian rights. We also have a principled reason for stopping at this point: It allows us to establish the resource community as *the* owner in terms of the Honoréan elements of ownership. By maintaining that the resource community has rights over its members' rights, what we are saying is that the member's claim-rights ultimately reside in, or are determined by, the community itself. We thereby also accomplish Waldron's goal of conceptualizing away cases in which ownership cannot be established due to the splitting or fragmentation of the property rights involved: In a common-property arrangement, the resource community is the entity to which its individual member's rights ultimately revert.

Furthermore, if we consider what actually happens when property or ownership is transferred from one entity to another, it is really the *rights*, rather than the things themselves, that are exchanged. As the economist Harold Demsetz writes, "When a transaction is conducted in the marketplace, *two bundles of property rights are exchanged*. A bundle of rights often attaches to a physical commodity or service, but it is the value of the rights that determines the value of what is exchanged."[50] If Eve simply hands an apple she owns to Adam, his mere possession of it does not, by itself, mean that he now owns it. All else being equal, he has no right to eat it, to sell it, or to throw it at a snake that is slithering by. However, Eve can transfer ownership of the apple to Adam while she still possesses it, and now he, not she, is the apple's owner. She no longer has any of the various rights of use vis-à-vis the apple she had only a moment ago; Adam now has them all. Establishing a common-property arrangement for water in the West would require individual appropriators to transfer *some* of their current powers or power rights to another entity, the resource community. But in doing so they would *not* have thereby transferred *all* of their rights to possess and use the resource. In other words, they would give up some of their rights of ownership, but they would not give up the thing itself, namely, the water. What have been transferred are, really, only certain rights of ownership.

In this section, I have offered an account of common-property arrangements in terms of the rights-relationship between individual resource users and the resource community to which they belong. The rights of the group's members are determined and limited by the collective choice of the members themselves qua their participation in the community's decisions. In such a state of affairs, though the members possess and use the resource, the community is, in an important sense, *the* owner because it determines the extent and content of the rights its members do have. The resource community owns the resource in virtue of its powers to manage how and by whom the resource is used.

THE NATURE OF RESOURCES AMENABLE TO COMMON-PROPERTY ARRANGEMENTS

Common-property arrangements are applicable only to a certain class of resources. In this section, I offer a set of conceptual tools, collectively termed "factor endowments," for analyzing the physical and technical attributes of such goods or resources. This class of resources amenable to a common-property arrangement includes things such as forests, rangeland, and water. The fact that in one setting such resources are controlled and managed as private property, in another as public property, in yet another as common property, and in some settings are instead open to anyone who wants to use them, implies that "there is no such thing as a common property *resource*; there are only resources controlled and managed as common property, or private property."[51] In other words, just because a resource has factor endowments that make it susceptible to a common-property arrangement does *not* mean that such an arrangement *should* be implemented. The brief analysis offered here is meant to be a heuristic tool for thinking through the logic of a situation and considering possible alternatives. The justification for favoring one rights-relationship alternative over another is the focus of the final three chapters.

Jointness

Employing several concepts culled from economics, we can identify the resources susceptible to common-property arrangements. The first of these factor endowments is jointness, which can be understood as the degree to which more than a single user can make use of the same good.[52] At one end of the jointness spectrum are those goods that any number of people can use without thereby interfering with each other or diminishing the resource in any appreciable way: no individual's use subtracts from the resource's overall benefit stream. At the other end are those goods that are literally consumed by a single individual: one person wholly uses up the capital of the thing. The former exhibit perfect jointness and are typically called pure public goods; the latter lack jointness altogether and are usually treated as private goods.[53]

I am not concerned with those goods that lack jointness altogether—an individual acorn, for example. While it is possible to have a common-property arrangement for a single acorn, it would be an impractical, perhaps even ludicrous, state of affairs. I take it for granted that such things are better managed and controlled as private property, or private goods.

Resources that exhibit perfect jointness are sometimes called open-access resources, but the two terms are neither synonymous nor coextensive: "Perfect jointness" refers to the *properties of the resource*; "open-access resource" primarily refers to the *properties of individuals' rights-relationship with one another*; the phrase "open-access resource" denotes a state of affairs where everyone has liberties to use the resource, and where there are no duties on any potential user to either use the resource or refrain from doing so. Both in theory and in fact, such a state of affairs may exist where perfect jointness does not, though probably not for long (see chapter 5). And even if a particular resource's benefit stream is not diminished by anyone's use, it may, however, be possible to improve the resource's overall benefit stream. In such cases, the establishment of property rights, not just liberties, may be justified. The most judicious arrangement of such rights, whether it is a private-, state-, or common-property arrangement, will depend very much on the goals of those in a position to use the resource. The main point here is that "pure public good" denotes a resource whose benefit stream is *unaffected* by any individual's use and can be used without diminution by any number of people. Think of the light from a street lamp. Although the street itself can become crowded, "the rate of consumption of the lamplight is independent of the number of consumers and of the particular use individuals make of the good (walking, jogging, motoring, or dancing in the streets)."[54] In such a situation, limiting the number of street-lamp users or controlling their uses via the assignment of property rights is rendered otiose.

It is only in situations where a resource is both susceptible to joint use and where such uses significantly affect the resource's benefit stream that a common-property arrangement may be in order. Some uses do not significantly affect the benefit stream of the resource—leaning against an apple tree to take a nap does not affect the tree's ability to produce apples. Some uses produce only temporary effects—picking an apple reduces the number of apples, but not the tree's capacity to produce more apples. Some uses are compatible *simultaneously*—I can pick apples off of the tree while you lean against it. And some uses are compatible *serially*—after your nap, I can use the tree to practice my knife throwing. The overall character of any property-rights arrangement for a particular resource will reflect the interplay of this complex of uses. Common-property arrangements are no exception.

Excludability

The second resource factor endowment is excludability, which refers, generally, to the degree to which access to the resource can be controlled.[55] Even where a resource is susceptible to joint uses that, either individually or collectively, significantly affect the resource's benefit stream, common-property arrangements may not make much sense. The power of management that vests in the resource community in such arrangements includes the power to determine both who can use the resource and how it can be used. If such exclusionary powers either cannot be enforced or can only be enforced with great expenditures of time and effort, then a common-property arrangement will be ineffectual in controlling resource use. The degree to which exclusion is attainable depends on both the physical nature of the resource and the available technology. Controlling access to a single tree is one thing—a dog and a shotgun would probably work; controlling access to an entire forest is another matter entirely—barbed wire, radar, and video cameras might well be enough though. Controlling access to a whole ocean or an entire three-thousand-mile national border, however, might well be next to impossible.

Only when it is possible to control effectively who has access to a resource will a common-property arrangement be effective for managing resource use. Yet even where access to the resource can be controlled, if the activities of individual resource users cannot be monitored and evaluated, then common-property arrangements may well prove ineffective. The jointness of a resource can be affected by the nature and complex of uses as much as it can be affected by the number of people using it. Therefore, being able to identify, separate, and then exclude some *uses*, either in whole or in part, that negatively affect the resource may be just as important as being able to identify, separate, and exclude *users*. In some situations, managing harmful uses may even shade into a requirement for productive use.

Where it is possible to monitor and control both users and uses, the high costs and ineffectiveness of such measures may prevent a common-property arrangement from developing. Private property, or even state ownership, may develop instead; the former may be cheaper in terms of overall social costs, and the latter may be more effective in terms of enforcement. The putative inability of common-property arrangements to deal effectively with such matters has been variously expressed as the "free rider problem" or "the tragedy of the commons." These matters will be taken up in some detail in chapter 5, where I argue that common-property arrangements need not succumb to such problems.

Indivisibility

In addition to exhibiting some measure of both jointness and excludability, resources amenable to common-property arrangements must also exhibit a certain measure of *indivisibility*. The indivisibility of a resource is mainly a question of scale, determined "by specifying the physical boundaries within which [it] cannot be divided without impairing its management potential or production value."[56] This factor endowment is better understood when viewed in two directions from one vantage point: looking outward from the resource community to nonmembers, and looking inward from the resource community to its members.

Certainly, if individuals are unable to physically mark off what is theirs, either individually or collectively, then excluding outsiders is hardly possible. It was not until the invention of barbed wire that western rangeland became susceptible to any form of property or ownership; until that invention, the rangeland was, for all intents and purposes, an open-access resource.[57] But resources are marked off and separated for various reasons and purposes, for example, for producing and extracting an income stream from the resource, or for maintaining the resource's physical integrity, continuity, or other attributes. Different property arrangements are no doubt better suited for different purposes, but one reason for preferring a common-property arrangement over private ownership may be that the former arrangement is better able to maintain the overall integrity, the quantity and quality, of resources like forests, rangeland, and rivers.[58] However, just controlling the physical boundaries of a forest, for instance, may not be enough to maintain its integrity. Pollution from nearby factories and cities, the draining of nearby wetlands, and all sorts of other actions by those outside the physical boundaries of the forest may undermine the community's goal of maintaining the integrity of the resource. This suggests that common-property arrangements will work well only when what the resource community can mark off is in some sense insulated from outside effects.[59] This outside-insulation factor is one way to understand and measure divisibility.

Assuming that the division just discussed is attainable, a further consideration is how the resource can be divided up among individual members of the resource community. If it is easy to split up, so that individuals can effectively manage and use separable bits of it, then the resource is highly divisible. If the resource cannot be easily split into separate or separable parcels, so that effective management and use requires more than one individual to be involved, then it is highly indivisible. Where the resource is hard to divide up, or where it can be divided up a variety of ways for a variety of different purposes, all of which might affect a resource's degrees of either jointness or excludability, a common-property arrangement may be feasible. Highly divisible resources are less amenable to common-property arrangements; they are most often better managed and controlled as private property.

So, the resources that may be well suited to a common-property arrangement have the following factor endowments: they are susceptible to joint use, and such usage has the potential for significantly affecting the resource's benefit stream; they exhibit a relatively low degree of excludability, such that one person's use often affects other users; and, finally, such resources exhibit a relatively high degree of indivisibility, so that even marking off what is mine from what is yours is not always a straightforward operation. These factor endowments will be articulated and refined in the following two chapters. The claim here is simply that resources having a high degree of both jointness and indivisibility and a low degree of excludability may be amenable to management by a group of users whose members decide, collectively, the extent and content of the group members' rights to possess and use the resource. It should be clear from the discussion in chapters 1 and 2 that water in the West fits this description, and, therefore, that the resource is a candidate, at least, for a common-property arrangement. The case must now be made that such an arrangement is, in fact, preferable to the sort of rights-relationship over water that exists in the West today.

In the next chapter, the concepts sketched earlier are further developed and used to analyze John Locke's account of property, or ownership, and to test its adequacy for a resource like water in the West. Some theorists have tried to apply Locke's account to the case of water in the West, but I argue that because he did not consider carefully enough the differences between resources, Locke overstated the desirability of private property for all scarce resources. And if Locke had thought more about the variability in resources' factor endowments, he may well have supported alternatives to private ownership for some resources, water included. In chapter 5, a further consideration of resources' factor endowments allows us to deflect more direct criticisms of common property, namely that all such arrangements will inevitably lead to a so-called tragedy of the commons. I argue that under certain conditions, a common-property arrangement may in fact be better than private ownership for preventing the depletion and degradation of a scarce resource, particularly one like water in the West.

NOTES

1. Lawrence C. Becker, *Property Rights: Philosophic Foundations* (London: Routledge and Kegan Paul, 1977), 190; see also Stephen P. Munzer, *A Theory of Property* (Cambridge: Cambridge University Press, 1990), 26.

2. See John W. Chapman, "Justice, Freedom, and Property," in *Property*, ed. J. Roland Pennock and John W. Chapman (New York: New York University Press, 1980), 289–324; see also Richard A. Epstein, "On the Optimal Mix of Private and Common Property," in *Property Rights*, ed. Ellen Frankel Paul, Fred D. Miller Jr., and Jeffery Paul (Cambridge: Cambridge University Press, 1994), 17–41.

3. N. Scott Arnold, "Economists and Philosophers as Critics of the Free Enterprise System," *The Monist* 73, no. 4 (October 1990): 633.

4. See Ronald J. Oakerson, "Analyzing the Commons: A Framework," in *Making the Commons Work*, ed. Daniel W. Bromley (San Francisco: Institute for Contemporary Studies, 1992), 46–47; S. V. Ciriacy-Wantrup and Richard C. Bishop, " 'Common Property' as a Concept in Natural Resources Policy," *Natural Resources Journal* 15, no. 4 (October 1975): 714–715; and Glenn G. Stevenson, *Common Property Economics: A General Theory and Land Use Applications* (Cambridge: Cambridge University Press, 1991), 39–46.

5. A. M. Honoré, "Ownership," in *Making Law Bind* (Oxford: Clarendon Press, 1987), 183.

6. Lawrence C. Becker, "The Moral Basis of Property Rights," in *Property*, ed. J. Roland Pennock and John W. Chapman (New York: New York University Press, 1980), 189–190.

7. See Wesley Newcomb Hohfeld, *Fundamental Legal Conceptions as Applied in Judicial Reasoning*, ed. Walter W. Cook (New Haven, CT: Yale University Press, 1919); and Becker, *Property Rights*, 7–14.

8. See Hohfeld, *Fundamental Legal Conceptions*, 35–41.

9. Hohfeld calls this a "privilege," though he admits that "liberty" would also suffice; Munzer adds that "freedom" might do just as well. See Hohfeld, *Fundamental Legal Conceptions*, 46–48; and Munzer, *Theory of Property*, 18.

10. Becker, *Property Rights*, 13.

11. Such forms of social pressure are taken up again and discussed more thoroughly in chapter 6.

12. Max Weber, *Economy and Society*, ed. Guenther Roth and Claus Wittich (Berkeley: University of California Press, 1968), 36.

13. Ibid., 34.

14. For a more detailed discussion of the distinction between legal and moral rights, see Becker, *Property Rights*, 16–17; H.L.A. Hart, *The Concept of Law* (Oxford: Oxford University Press, 1961), 54–60, 163–180; and Weber, *Economy and Society*, 24–36.

15. Honoré, "Ownership," 162.

16. Ibid., 166. Honoré qualifies "physical control" by adding "or to have such control as the nature of the thing admits." Even with this qualification, however, it seems clear that the object of ownership for Honoré must be material or be materially based. This requirement complicates discussion of the ownership of *nonmaterial* things, like intellectual property. While a discussion of property rights over nonmaterial things is beyond the scope of this book, a few points are worth mentioning. It is highly profitable to at least start with material things, and the case has been made that ideas are recorded on patent documents and the like, so that in a not insignificant sense there is a material basis for such things. See Munzer, *Theory of Property*, chapter 3. Becker takes a different tack: "Where the thing is non-corporeal, possession may be understood metaphorically." See Becker, "Moral Basis of Property Rights," 190; see also Jeremy Waldron, *The Right to Private Property* (Oxford: Clarendon Press, 1988), 33–37.

17. Becker, *Property Rights*, 21.

18. Ibid.

19. There is an intimate connection between the right to possess and the right to use, or more generally, between possession and use. Honoré's insistence that the right to possess is the foundation upon which everything else is built might be taken to imply that use entails possession. While this is most often the case, it is not always so. The right to the income from my desk can be considered a use even though someone else may be in physical possession of it. Also, I can use my television while only possessing the remote. Perhaps we can extend the definition of "television" to include the remote, and thereby avoid this difficulty. However, the case where I receive income from a thing that is clearly not under my physical control suggests that use need not entail possession.

20. Robert Nozick, *Anarchy, State, and Utopia* (New York: Basic, 1974), 171.

21. Honoré, "Ownership," 168–169, emphasis added.

22. See Becker, "Moral Basis of Property Rights," 191.

23. Waldron, *Right to Private Property*, 49.

24. See Nozick, *Anarchy, State, and Utopia*, 171.

25. With regard to water rights under the doctrine of prior appropriation, we might note here several peculiarities. Under that doctrine, the duty to prevent harmful use shades into a *duty to use* the water productively. Similarly, the liberty to use the water shades into or becomes a *duty to use* it productively as well. One loses one's rights to the water if it is not so used. Therefore, one is liable to execution of one's water rights in the

West not only for failure to pay a debt, but also for simply failing to use it productively.

26. Becker, *Property Rights*, 21.

27. See Becker, "Moral Basis of Property Rights," 191.

28. Waldron, *Right to Private Property*, 38–39, emphasis added.

29. See Stephen P. Munzer, *A Theory of Property*, 25; and Waldron, *Right to Private Property*, 57; see also Ciriacy-Wantrup and Bishop, "Common Property," 714.

30. Honoré, "Ownership," 168.

31. Thomas C. Grey, "The Disintegration of Property," in *Property*, ed. J. Roland Pennock and John W. Chapman (New York: New York University Press, 1980), 81.

32. For a detailed criticism of Grey's position, see Munzer, *Theory of Property*, 31–36.

33. See Honoré, "Ownership," 172.

34. Becker, "Moral Basis of Property Rights," 192.

35. Becker, *Property Rights*, 20.

36. Becker, "Moral Basis of Property Rights," 192.

37. Waldron, *Right to Private Property*, 39.

38. Ibid., 41.

39. Ibid., 45.

40. Douglas North and Robert P. Thomas, "The First Economic Revolution," *Economic History Review* 30 (1977): 234.

41. See Becker, *Property Rights*, 25.

42. Munzer, *Theory of Property*, 25.

43. Oakerson, "Analyzing the Commons," 47.

44. Waldron, *Right to Private Property*, 39.

45. See Daniel W. Bromley, *Environment and Economy: Property Rights and Public Policy* (Oxford: Basil Blackwell, 1991), 25; and Stevenson, *Common Property Economics*, 57.

46. Oakerson, "Analyzing the Commons," 47, emphasis added.

47. Honoré, "Ownership," 168–169. When he goes on to discuss, briefly, cases of split ownership, he is primarily concerned with the social function of such states of affair, and identifies two types of situations when splitting the elements of ownership may be in order. Splitting the rights of ownership may work "towards continuity by maintaining in being a physical thing . . . that it may serve [an] association over a substantial period." Alternatively, "splitting may serve the purpose of specialization, by separating management from the enjoyment [of the thing]. The person who is entitled to the benefit thus obtains the advantage of expert management but also runs some risk." Ibid., 188. No doubt the risk here is that the experts might determine that some uses should be curtailed or stopped altogether. Thus, we see that the need to manage scarce resources might require the *insecurity* of individual's use rights. See also chapter 2.

48. Waldron, *Right to Private Property*, 56.

49. Honoré, "Ownership," 183.

50. Harold Demsetz, "Toward a Theory of Property Rights," *American Economic Review: Papers and Proceedings* 57 (1967): 347, emphasis added.

51. Bromley, *Environment and Economy*, 2, emphasis in original.

52. See Oakerson, "Analyzing the Commons," 44.

53. In fact, Paul Samuelson introduced the term "jointness" into economics in 1954 to describe pure public goods. The way I am employing the term here, as a variable referring to the "subtractibility" of individual's uses, is of a more recent vintage. See Oakerson, "Analyzing the Commons," 43–44.

54. Oakerson, "Analyzing the Commons," 41.

55. Ibid.

56. Ibid., 45.

57. See Terry L. Anderson and P. J. Hill, "From Free Grass to Fences: Transforming the Commons of the American West," in *Managing the Commons*, ed. Garrett Hardin and John Baden (New York: Freeman, 1977), 207–208.

58. See Honoré, "Ownership," 188; and Bromley, *Environment and Economy*, 2.

59. Or a common-property arrangement may work where those individuals outside the resource boundaries can be included in the resource community. Outside individuals may also include those individuals who are within the resource boundaries but who do use the resource.

4

Locke's Account of Property

Though the Water running in the Fountain be every ones, yet who can doubt, but that in the Pitcher is his only who drew it out. His *labour* hath taken it out of the hands of Nature, where it was common, and belong'd equally to all her Children, and *hath* thereby *appropriated* it to himself.

No Body could think himself injur'd by the drinking of another Man, though he took a good Draught, who had a whole River of the same Water left him to quench his thirst. And the Case of Land and Water, where there is enough of both, is perfectly the same.

John Locke, *Second Treatise of Government*

INTRODUCTION

Many philosophers dismiss John Locke's account of property because they believe its premises to be wildly unrealistic and its implications largely irrelevant.[1] However, some historians and economists have recently argued that Locke's account, in fact, provides the descriptive and normative basis for the current structure of water rights in the American West. Alfred Z. Cuzán, for example, writes that Locke's account "explains the way water in fact was appropriated under nearly anarchical conditions in the West during the mid-nineteenth century."[2] And he goes on to argue, "Locke would not have found the commercialization of water irreverent or objectionable in any way."[3]

Cuzán is among a group of economists who believe that water in the West should be treated like any other commodity, subject to appropriation and exchange in a market economy. "An economist," Timothy D. Tregarthen writes, "might be defined as someone who doesn't see anything special about water." [4] For a market to work effectively, individuals must have secure, exclusive, and transferable rights to that water, that is, extensive private property rights.[5] The implication here is that Locke saw nothing special about water either, and that he, like Cuzán and Tregarthen, would have found it legitimate for individuals to have extensive private property rights over water.

Although I agree that Locke saw nothing special about water, I do not agree that he would have necessarily supported extensive private property rights over it. Locke says very little about water—the previous quotes represent virtually all he has to say about it—and when he does mention it he treats it just like any other external good.[6] Others have already noted in passing that Locke makes almost no distinction at all between various kinds of external goods or resources.[7] Locke, of course, recognizes that there are structural and functional differences between resources, but he does not explore those differences carefully enough. This is unfortunate; it causes him to write as if the rules of property that arise will quite naturally be the same for all resources. However, as I will argue later in this chapter, the rules of property or ownership applicable to a particular resource very much depend on its factor endowments—its degrees of jointness, excludability, and divisibility. For some resources it makes sense to promote the full range of private property rights, for others it might make more sense to limit those rights. Locke gives insufficient attention to variations in resources' factor endowments; he operates with a largely monochromatic and rather hazy picture of the nature of resources. Although his account of property begins with things like acorns, apples, and other perishable goods, it seems clear enough that it is property rights in *land* and other nonperishable means of production with which he is most concerned.[8] He first attempts to justify a certain set of property rights for the former sorts of goods, and he then goes on to argue, by analogy, for the same set of rights in the latter kind. This move, I maintain, is not well grounded because there *are* significant differences, both among perishable goods and between them and nonperishable goods. Locke sees no difference between the cases of water and land; they are, he says, "perfectly the same."[9] But they are in fact quite different, and this suggests that different sets of rights may be justified for different sorts of resources. I argue that the structure of Locke's arguments about the extent and content of property rights leaves room for different rights-arrangements for different resources. If Locke had attended more carefully to the variable nature of resources, he may well have objected to extensive private property rights for some of them, including water.

What is the structure of Locke's arguments for private property rights? If Locke was indeed the source for thinking about resources for those who first appropriated water in the West, and if some economists want to implicate him in justifications for water rights today, then they must read him primarily as a consequentialist about property rights—that is, someone who argues that the extent and content of property rights are justified by their usefulness to particular purposes or ends. Under the western doctrine of prior appropriation, the first person who puts water to productive use thereby gains secure, exclusive, and transferable rights over it. That person can lose those rights only if he or she stops using the water altogether.[10] Westerners originally adopted this doctrine in the 1840s because it supported rapid settlement in and economic development of an unpopulated and inhospitable region. The doctrine, as one historian puts it, "seemed to be natural to a group of people who were intent on conquering, expanding, accumulating, and getting ahead."[11] Economists who today support the doctrine of prior appropriation do so because they believe in the virtues of the marketplace, and they believe as well that secure, exclusive, and transferable rights are necessary for markets to function effectively.[12] Both the settlers then and these economists today justify private property rights because they are useful for particular purposes or ends: rapidly developing the arid West, efficiently utilizing a now-scarce resource, and so on. For Locke to be the source of this approach, it must be possible to read him as justifying private property rights for the same sorts of reasons: because those rights are useful for important purposes and ends.

Locke's arguments for private property rights can indeed be read in this way. His theory of property has often been read otherwise: as being inextricably bound up with theocentric notions; as being duty-based or desert-based; and as being driven by deontological rather than consequentialist concerns.[13] But I think that Locke can be read as a political (and moral) pluralist, someone who offers diverse and independent lines of argument for his conclusions. I agree with A. John Simmons's assessment that such pluralism "does much to explain the incredibly wide range of interpretations . . . offered in the scholarly literature [on Locke]."[14] My intent here is not to offer a comprehensive interpretation of Locke's view of property. Rather, it is to counter Cuzán's claim that Locke, *read as a consequentialist*, would necessarily come to the conclusion that it is not at all objectionable for individuals to have extensive private property rights in a resource like western water. I maintain that there is room within a consequentialist reading of Locke for coming to a different conclusion.

Accordingly, in this chapter I begin by arguing that the extent and content of property rights are justified for Locke by how useful they are, to both individuals and their society as a whole. Most of what he says about property rights concerns how they first might arise in a "state of nature," at a time when the world's resources were unowned and relatively abundant, and when there was no established law or government. Under such conditions, it is legitimate, Locke thinks, for individuals to use whatever resources they need, so long as they do not waste any. *Waste*, I maintain, is the primary constraint on the extent and content of property rights in Locke's state of nature; wasting things is simply antithetical to our purpose, which, Locke writes, is "to make use of [resources] to the best advantage of life."[15] Locke justifies the rise of private property rights in the state of nature by arguing that when individuals have such rights, less of the world's resources will be wasted.

The injunction against waste also affects property rights after the initial conditions justifying them have changed. Although most of what Locke says about property in external goods concerns how they originally might be appropriated in a state of nature, he is aware that changes in those circumstances may well require changes in the extent and content of individuals' property rights. According to Locke, individuals leave the state of nature when they consent to join together into a commonwealth and agree to be governed by civil authorities.[16] His scattered remarks about the powers for "regulating," "determining," and "settling" property vested in the civil authorities imply that property rights are legitimately subject to modification once people are no longer in a state of nature.[17] He thinks that the main motivation for such modification will be the emergence of scarcity, but he says little about how such scarcity will actually affect individuals' property rights.[18] When a resource, especially a vital one like water, becomes scarce, it seems only reasonable to try to waste as little of it as possible. All of this suggests that any changes in the extent and content of property rights after people have left the state of nature will be justified in large part because those changes will reduce waste.

My overarching thought here is this: It seems reasonable to maintain that property rights should be proportioned to the purposes they serve.[19] Locke, I argue, held just this sort of position. Given their instrumental character, it is possible that property rights may vary justifiably as purposes for and uses of those resources themselves vary. Although Locke understood this too, he did not actually consider how variations in resources' factor endowments support variations in property rights, either in a state of nature or when individuals have later quit that state. If we examine the structure of Locke's arguments justifying property rights, we can see how and why he thought that private property rights would allow individuals to use the world's resources to the best advantage of life. If we then attend to the ways in which resources' factor endowments actually do vary, we can see that there is room within Locke's account of property for other rights-arrangements. Simply put, it is consistent with Locke's view that as resources become scarce users should rethink how those resources are used. Locke, in other words, would grant that where our purposes can be better served through different rights-arrangements, it is legitimate to restrict or rearrange individuals' property rights.

THE EXTENT AND CONTENT OF PROPERTY RIGHTS

The problem Locke sets for himself in chapter 5 of the *Second Treatise of Government* is to give a descriptive and normative account of how individuals can come to have "a *Property* in any thing" in the state of nature.[20] By "any thing," he means primarily external goods, such as the products of the earth, for example, food and water, and parts of the earth itself, for example, land. What Locke means by "a property in" such things, though, is not so straightforward, and giving an account of what he means and how he goes about justifying it is the main burden of this section. What *is* clear in Locke is that one's property in a thing, whatever it might consist of, derives from one's productive *use* of that thing. He gives three arguments justifying individuals' use of resources that they find in the state of nature.

The first argument Locke uses begins with his belief that we are naturally driven to preserve ourselves.[21] Since our preservation requires food, water, and other resources, we must use such things. In order to use them we must first *change* them; we must in some way *alter* things from how we initially find them. Apples and acorns must be gathered and deer and rabbits must be captured before they can be of any use to our preservation. Such things are useless as we find

them initially. Locke asserts that in the beginning, everything belonged "to Mankind in common," by which he means that everyone
had an equal liberty to use or alter things.[22] Our liberty to perform
acts of alteration, when combined with our need to do so in order to
survive, gives us a prima facie justification for doing so. We are justified in using things productively because we need to do so in order to
preserve ourselves. This can be called the "need" argument.

Locke's second argument justifying the use of unowned resources
in the state of nature relies on the putative fact that everything is,
initially, so abundant that no one's use harms or is otherwise prejudicial to anyone else. He says:

> Considering the plenty of natural Provisions there was a long
> time in the world, and the few spenders, and to how small a part
> of that provision the industry of one Man could extend it self,
> and ingross it to the prejudice of others; especially keeping
> within the *bounds*, set by reason of what might serve for his *use*;
> there could be then little room for Quarrels or Contentions
> about Property so established.[23]

Where my use of some thing does *not negatively affect* you, it is *per-
missible* for me to use it. Though I am using *this* apple or *this* rabbit
or *this* mouthful of water, other such items are readily available for
your use, so you should not have any quarrel with me; my use of the
resource does not materially affect you. This can be called the "why
not?" argument.[24]

In his third argument, Locke justifies using unowned resources in
the state of nature because of the overall good such use brings about:
"He who appropriates land to himself by his labour, does not lessen
but *increase the common stock* of mankind."[25] His thought here is
that certain alterations to a resource, for example, tilling and planting land, make more of that resource available to others. Locke
thinks that if an individual relied on hunting and gathering, then
that individual would need to use a hundred acres of land in order to
survive. However, if that individual practiced cultivation, then he or
she would need only ten acres. Thus, Locke concludes, he who tills
and plants land "may truly be said, to give ninety acres to Mankind."[26] Here, then, we have an argument, when generalized, that some
uses of some resources actually have *positive effects on others*, bene-
fiting them by providing them with resources that would not otherwise be available to them. If your use of a resource benefits me, then
not only should I refrain from quarreling over your use, I should ac-

tually encourage it. This can be called the "benefit to others" argument. Locke thinks it is part of human nature for individuals to have
some concern for others' preservation and well being, so that when
my own preservation and well being is not threatened, I "naturally"
will be moved by the fact that my use of a resource might help others
to preserve themselves.[27]

For Locke, then, it is legitimate for individuals to use resources in
the state of nature: they need to use them; such use is not prejudicial
to others; and such use may even be beneficial to others. But property
for Locke is more than simply having the *liberty* of using things. A
necessary feature of property for Locke is its immunity from expropriation: "I have truly no *Property* in that which another can by right
take from me, when he pleases, against my consent."[28] That is, when
I have property in something, I have an exclusive *right* to use it and
others have a concomitant *duty* to refrain from using it or from stopping me from using it, provided I do not harm others via that use.[29]
How on Locke's account does the *liberty* to use a resource become an
exclusive *claim-right* over it?

Locke starts from the assumption that everyone has exclusive
claim-rights over themselves and, by extension, over their own *labor*:
"every Man has a *Property* in his own person. This no Body has any
right to but himself. The *Labour* of his Body, and the *Work* of his
hands, we may say, are properly his."[30] From this supposition, Locke
thinks that there is a straightforward argument to the conclusion
that one acquires exclusive claim-rights to that with which one
mixes one's labor. One has claim-rights to one's labor, and when one
"mixes" one's labor with some object, it becomes "infused" with those
claim-rights. A person mixes his or her labor with an object by using
it, thereby appropriating it and making it "a part of him, that another can no longer have any right to it."[31] So, Locke is arguing that
individuals have liberties to use things, and because they can use
things only by *laboring* on them, they thereby appropriate or *incorporate* those things into themselves; hence, they legitimately acquire
claim-rights over them. Since individuals can legitimately use resources in the state of nature, they can justifiably come to have
claim-rights over them too.

If we take "incorporation" here in a broad and figurative sense,
then we can understand laboring, not as some mysterious substance
that is somehow mixed with things, but as *an activity aimed at productive use*. We do not literally mix our bodies with things or vice
versa (except when we eat things); rather, we incorporate things into
our productive activities, or our life plans. Laboring is any activity

intended to either use things or make them useful. This picture accords well with Simmons's recent characterization of what constitutes "laboring" for Locke: "any kind of purposive activity aimed at satisfying needs or supplying the conveniences of life."[32] Reading Locke this way mitigates against infelicitous aspects of the mixing metaphor he relies on when discussing gathering and hunting,[33] and as we shall see, this reading also allows us to make sense of the natural limits Locke imposes on an individual's claim-rights over resources. Labor should not be thought of as some pseudosubstance that is mixed with acorns, rabbits, and the like when we touch them, but more generally as a readily recognizable way of *using* such things with the intent of bringing them, or incorporating them, into our life plans.[34] The gathering or the hunting constitutes not the use itself, but the *intent* to use the thing. It is an activity *aimed at* use.

Thinking of laboring, generally, as engaging in purposive, productive activity aimed at bringing things into one's life plans also allows us to understand how Locke can extend the notion of labor to activities where the mixing metaphor is remote and difficult to maintain. By enclosing some parcel of land with a fence, for instance, one thereby signals one's intent of using all the enclosed land, and not just the area beneath the fence posts. No physical touching of the enclosed land has occurred. More generally, " 'tis the taking any part of what is common and removing it out of the state Nature leaves it in, which begins the Property, without which the Common is of no use."[35] Diverting water from a river, though an activity not considered by Locke, operates in the same way. One diverts water from a river with the intent of using it, but one actually *labors* on the banks of the river in order to effect such diversion. The diverted water, like the land inside the fence, is an indirect product of one's labor; the water is given value by one's labor or removal, but one's labor is not mixed with the water in any straightforward way. It may be possible to argue that when a farmer tills the land, or when he or she *uses* the diverted water by irrigating crops with it, *that* activity constitutes mixing one's labor with the resource. But one's *property in* something begins before such activity; it begins, for Locke, at "the taking," which is a precondition for the using. This taking is a signal of incorporating such things, not literally into one's body, but rather into one's life plans. It is a purposive activity that does not itself satisfy our needs, but that is aimed at such satisfaction.

It is an open question whether this is the most perspicacious way to read Locke's arguments regarding labor. Clearly, however, Cuzán relies on something like this reading to describe the development of the western doctrine of prior appropriation. In reference to Locke's comments about water in a pitcher belonging to whoever drew it out, Cuzán notes that it is "the act of *removing* a portion of the commons [that] establishes an individual's property over it, eliminating the ambiguity associated with the concept of 'mixing' one's labor with the earth."[36] The thrust of Cuzán's subsequent discussion is that it makes no difference whether this removal is by means of dipping a pitcher into a fountain or by cutting a diversion ditch into the banks of a river.

Historical evidence suggests that, prior to any overt attempt by western settlers to coordinate their behavior, such removals and diversions were seen by subsequent settlers as legitimate acts of appropriation, conferring on the first user claim-rights to that water. Before either statutory laws for or civil authority over water had been established in the western territory, "if an individual found a stream [being used], he simply moved on to another water supply."[37] The fact is that once an individual was engaged in purposive activities and was using water to further those activities, others respected those activities and uses. Secure, exclusive rights to use water in the West arose under conditions resembling Locke's state of nature, and they arose by an apparently prosaic process whereby the productive activities of individuals were recognized and respected by others.

For Locke, a sufficient condition for the state of nature is the lack of a commonly agreed upon authority.[38] In describing the state of nature, he posits it to be populated by morally sophisticated individuals, who can make and keep various promises or agreements: "For Truth and keeping of Faith belongs to Men, as Men, and not as Members of Society."[39] In recognizing and respecting one another's use of resources, individuals do not thereby leave the state of nature, for "'tis not every Compact that puts an end to the State of Nature, but only this one of agreeing together to enter into one Community, and make one Body Politick."[40] So it is possible for individuals to recognize one another's claim-rights prior to agreeing that some civil authority can legitimately enforce—and perhaps modify—those rights.

Regardless of skepticism about the cogency of Locke's arguments for *why* laboring on some thing produces claim-rights in it, recognizing that laborers have at least some property rights in at least some of the things they produce appears to be a universal practice. As Lawrence C. Becker observes, "It seems that all recorded societies recognize *in practice* laborers' entitlements to ... simple productive goods the laborers have produced."[41] Becker takes the universality of this practice to imply its naturalness. In looking for a nonarbitrary starting point for moral argument, starting with what human beings actually and universally do, although it is not incontestable, seems at least a cogent approach; if nothing else, it shifts the burden of proof to those who would argue against such practices. So, however badly Locke defends the view that laboring on some thing gives the laborer a special claim to it, he nonetheless appears to be on to something. The universality of the practice speaks to the reasonableness of maintaining that, in the absence of either express consent or explicit coordination, people could recognize one another as having legitimate property rights in what they have labored on.

Such recognition is both possible and likely where there is no question about what constitutes one's laboring. The first examples of laboring in the state of nature Locke offers are the basic, primitive ones of gathering and hunting. He clearly assumes that such actions on one's part would naturally signal to others one's intent of *using* the things thereby "produced"—grabbing and gobbling are the most basic of survival activities, and they are the simplest and most direct ways in which we use the earth's resources. There may be some question as to *when*, exactly, such and such an activity qualifies as a purposive and useful activity, but Locke sees no such determination problems with at least the basic activities like gathering and hunting: the acorn is useful, that is, has value, when it is in my hand; the water is useful when it is in my pitcher; the rabbit is useful when I kill it—"who can doubt" such things, Locke says.[42] Later, conventions might be established that expand or constrict what is to count as gathering, and so on, but no express or tacit agreements are needed for the basic cases Locke has in mind. In short, no formal agreements are necessary, Locke thinks, in order for people to recognize and understand gathering and hunting as laboring. And once others see the labor in some thing, the recognition of at least some property rights in that thing seems a likely occurrence.

So far, I have argued that Locke offers three arguments—need, why not?, and benefit to others—to show why people have liberties to use external goods in the state of nature. And *duties* to respect other's uses arise in that state because individuals recognize one another's laboring as productive activity aimed at satisfying his or her needs. It is the presence of such duties that signals the presence of claim-rights, and it is the presence of claim-rights with respect to external goods that marks at least *some* form of property or ownership. However, we need to examine these claim-rights in more detail before we can understand the form of property Locke is trying to justify.

One source of confusion and controversy in interpreting the extent and content of property rights in Locke is that he tries both to justify property rights and to defend limits to those rights at the same time. The result, I maintain, is a *limited* form of private property. It is the limitations on the extent and content of property rights over resources in the state of nature that, primarily, sets the stage for legitimately reconfiguring those rights if and when those resources become moderately scarce.

Locke justifies limits on property rights by employing two requirements or constraints. He says that there must be "enough, and as good left in common for others," and he says that nothing should "spoil" or go to waste.[43] These constraints have been seen as not only resulting in different limits, but also as jointly failing to regulate adequately the transition from the commons to private ownership. The reasons adduced for this failure are encapsulated by Richard A. Epstein: the first constraint "binds too tightly [because once] the initial appropriator removes anything from the commons, how can there be as much left as before"; and the second constraint "does not bind at all" because, since an individual who removes things from the commons must pay some positive costs in terms of labor, and so on, "he will only convert common property to private property when his gains exceed his costs."[44] That is, no external constraints are required because, by pragmatic reasoning alone, individuals would not intentionally waste their labor by working harder than they had to. There are, however, good reasons for thinking that the no-waste constraint alone serves to bound property rights for Locke in the state of nature. First, however, let us briefly consider the "enough and as good left" requirement.

The enough and as good left requirement should not be taken as a constraint on original appropriation at all. Rather, Locke saw it as being a material *fact* about appropriation in the state of nature: "Considering the plenty of natural Provisions there was a long time in the World, and the few spenders, and to how small a part of that provision the industry of one Man could extend to himself and ingross it to the prejudice of others . . . there could be then little room for Quarrels."[45] This is part of the why not? argument I discussed earlier. For Locke, the enough and as good left requirement simply does not come into play under conditions of abundance encountered in the state of nature. It influences property rights only when resources become scarce. If we focus, then, on the fact that Locke is primarily concerned with original appropriation in a state of natural abundance, it seems that the justification for limiting individuals' property rights must rely on the no-waste constraint alone.

In order to understand how the no-waste constraint functions in the justification of property rights, I want to first briefly lay out the rights I take Locke to be defending. The property rights in external goods Locke is most centrally concerned to justify in the state of nature can be described, generally, as the rights of use.[46] Now use can be understood either narrowly or broadly. In the narrowest sense, it means only personal use of the thing; in a broader sense, it includes foregoing personal use and allowing others to use it instead. For example, it includes both the right to its income and the right to its alienation (transfer, sale, or bequeathal). It is personal use of resources that Locke thinks is required for one's preservation. But he also allows for uses beyond this bare minimum; he recognizes that individuals can use things for what he calls the "Conveniencies of Life," those above and beyond what one requires for one's survival.[47] Furthermore, Locke allows that individuals can use some things indirectly, by trading or bartering with others.[48] It seems clear, then, that Locke intends use in a broad sense, and that he wants to defend the rights concomitant with use so understood.

Using a thing might well require physically modifying it, including completely consuming it, using it up, or destroying it. Such actions constitute using up the capital of the thing. The right to use up the capital of things seems to be an integral part of the right to use them, regardless of whether use is conceived of narrowly or broadly.[49] Remembering that we are concerned here only with rights over external goods, and not with those (property) rights one might have over one's body, it is clear that Locke wants to defend one's right to use up the capital of a thing. He says, "Property . . . is for the benefit and sole Advantage of the Proprietor, so that he may even destroy the thing, that he has Property in by his use of it, where need requires."[50]

If we understand the no-waste constraint as a corollary to our purposive activities, then we can see how the rights of property just adduced are both generated and logically constrained in Locke's account. But first we need to examine briefly Locke's notion of waste. Although he says that something is wasted whenever it spoils, decays, or perishes without being gathered,[51] this is neither entirely correct nor wholly concordant with Locke's intentions. If he had considered more carefully the variety of ways things could be used productively, I think that he would have had to revise this too-facile description of waste. For instance, lots of things can be wasted, that is, not incorporated into our purposive activities, even though they do not spoil or decay in the way Locke implies. For example, a desk can be wasted either by frivolously destroying it or by leaving it in the corner of one's attic with no intention of ever using it again. Also, external goods are a part of our productive activities when we use them productively, and some productive uses actually do involve letting things spoil—some foods and medicines are made in this way— or perish without being gathered—some agricultural practices involve exactly this technique. So, although Locke seems to equate such activities with waste, he could not, I think, have intended to admonish them.

One possible source for Locke's confusion here is his contention that "the greatest part of *things really useful* to the Life of Man, . . . *are* generally things of short duration; such as, if they are not consumed by use, will decay and perish of themselves."[52] But even this is not true for all "really useful" things, that is, things we need to preserve ourselves; land need not decay or perish of itself, at least not in any straightforward way. Locke does think that "Land that is left wholly to Nature, that hath no improvement of Pasturage, Tillage, or Planting, is called, as indeed it is, *waste*; and we shall find the benefit of it amount to little more than nothing."[53] However, in the contemporary world we *have* found great value in and reaped many benefits from land left wholly to nature. It is useful precisely because it is *not* consumed by use. In any case, while Locke might have inadvertently suggested that certain activities (or inactivities, e.g., not using things) signify waste, a view more in line with his intent is that something is wasted either if it is not being used productively or if there is no intent on the possessor's part to so use it.

So, the right to the capital of a thing, the right to income from it, and the right to alienate it are all justified in the state of nature because they are an integral part of what Locke sees as the general right to use that thing. An individual's use of a resource, via his or her labor, generates claim-rights over that resource. Using some thing means for Locke incorporating that thing into one's purposive activities. Such incorporation necessarily encompasses modifying those things from how one finds them originally, and such modification may include destroying those things or exchanging them for other things one might need or want instead. As they are found in the state of nature, all resources are wasted *absolutely*, in the sense that none of them are useful at all. In such a state of affairs, any individual's use of a resource reduces this waste.

Locke's justification of property rights, however, is conditional. He believes that removing something from the commons via one's labor gives that person a right only to what he or she can make *use* of. With regard to land, Locke writes:

> Whatsoever he tilled and reaped, laid up and *made use of*, before it spoiled, that was his particular Right; whatsoever he enclosed, and could feed, and *make use of*, the Cattle and Product was also his. But if either the Grass of his Inclosure rotted on the Ground, or the Fruit of his planting perished without gathering ... notwithstanding his Inclosure, was still to be looked on as *Waste*, and might be the Possession of any other.[54]

A person wastes something when he or she either fails to use it productively or has no intention of ever doing so. According to Locke, if I waste something in my possession, then, I no longer have any rights over it, and anyone is at liberty to make use of it instead. Claim-rights over a resource begin and end for Locke with one's productive use of that resource. Although labor serves to begin the process of productive use, *waste* serves as the limit to the claim-rights engendered by that labor. (We should remember that under the western doctrine of prior appropriation, rights to one's water are lost if one stops using it.)

In a state of affairs where using things is both necessary and not prejudicial to others, using things in *any* way is better than not using them at all: Since everything, at first, is wasted, any use will reduce that absolute waste. This we get from the need and why not? arguments. Where an individual's use of a resource makes more of it available to others, *those* uses are preferred. This we get from the benefit to others argument: It is preferable, Locke says, for land to be enclosed and cultivated, rather than wandered upon for hunting and gathering, *because* cultivation increases the "common stock of mankind." Among the land-use options available (hunting, gathering, and cultivation), cultivation is to the better advantage of everyone. If more land will be enclosed and cultivated by securing to individuals private property rights, then it is only pragmatic for individuals to recognize and respect those rights.[55] Cultivating land is relatively less wasteful than some other activities.

More generally, the structure of Locke's argument implies that failing to use a scarce resource efficiently is tantamount to wasting it: If there is a relatively less wasteful way to use the resource, then *that* use is preferable. When a resource is scarce, inefficient or wasteful uses of it should be discouraged. If land were scarce, and if some people were still subsisting on the fruits and nuts they gathered up from the ground, then more land could be made available to others if those gatherers would become cultivators instead. In that case, gathering is more wasteful than another available option, and we would want to discourage gathering in favor of cultivating. One way to discourage an activity is to point out its relative disadvantage. In answer to the question, "Why shouldn't I use this resource in this way?" one could reasonably reply, "Well, because there is not enough of it, and there is a way for you to use it that makes more of it available for others." That is, one can use the benefit to others argument as a legitimate reply to the why not? argument. If a group of people were concerned about getting the most value out of a scarce resource, then they might well find it unreasonable for an individual to use that resource in a relatively wasteful way. In that case, they may *not* recognize an individual's rights to continue to use that resource in *that* way. More generally, where a scarce resource is susceptible to several uses that may each have differing effects on others, the extent and content of property rights recognized by others may vary with those uses. Later on, I discuss this variability in a resource's jointness and argue that resources that display a high degree of jointness are sometimes ill suited to private ownership.

Resources need not be scarce for such considerations to come into play; the no-waste constraint affects the extent and content of property rights even where a resource is abundant. The injunction against waste, conceived of as including both absolute and relative waste, suggests that, all else being equal, laboring less is preferable to laboring more. Locke describes laboring as involving some costs to the laborer: he who removes things from the commons necessarily takes "pains about it."[56] Obviously, individuals would prefer to take fewer pains than more; they would prefer to expend as little labor costs as they needed to. This cost-efficient, or pragmatic, thinking will naturally constrain how much of the commons individuals do in fact appropriate. This is no doubt why Epstein maintains that the no-waste constraint does not bind at all: People in the state of nature simply will not waste things, if for no other reason than that it is impractical or inefficient for them to do so. Not only will they appropriate only what they can use, he thinks, but they will use those resources in the most cost-efficient and pragmatic way they can.[57] It may well be the case, however, that for some resources, less labor and more benefit can be achieved by limiting the extent and content of rights individuals have over that resource. If that were true—and in the next section I argue that it is—then it would be legitimate to recognize more limited property rights in the state of nature even for abundant resources.

I have been arguing that the structure of Locke's arguments quite easily accommodates limits to the rights of use if those limits result in less waste. This relies on understanding waste as having something to do with the relative advantage of different uses, but I think Locke can be understood as using waste in this way. He says that reason tells us not only to use things, but to use them "to the best advantage of Life," and it is not only our own lives with which we should be concerned, but also those of "mankind" generally: Reason tells us that "when [a man's] own Preservation comes not in competition, ought he, as much as he can, *to preserve the rest of Mankind.*"[58] This suggests that, all else being equal, we should use things in ways that are better for the preservation of everyone.

As I noted earlier, Locke also makes a distinction between resources used for one's survival and those used for one's less-pressing conveniences. He says that in a situation where two individuals are each trying to use a scarce resource, the one with the more pressing need should be given preference: "The Fundamental Law of Nature being, that all, as much as may be, should be preserved, it follows that if there be not enough to satisfy both . . . , he that hath, and to spare, must remit something of his full Satisfaction, and give way to the pressing and preferable Title of those, who are in danger to perish without it."[59] Locke thinks that when the *convenience* of some people conflicts with the *preservation* and survival of others, it is *better*, all things considered, for the former to give some of what they have to the latter. If this is correct, then "better" or "less wasteful" is not meant by Locke to be synonymous with "more productive" construed in narrow economic terms, for example, more profitable or efficient, generating more income, better for the gross national product, and so on. Rather, what is better is whatever works toward the good "of every person" or the "preservation of the whole."[60] This suggests that what is best in terms of one's labor costs may not be what is best for everyone; the best use of a thing may not be the most efficient use. It might well cost me more labor if I remit to you something which I could live without but which you could not; nonetheless, it seems reasonable to do so on Locke's account. And insofar as the structure of property rights should work to everyone's preservation, such rights may legitimately be restricted so that one person's needs are attended to before another person's mere conveniences.

In summary, I have argued that, for Locke, people come to have claim-rights to use external goods or resources by incorporating them into their purposive activities. These rights include the right to the capital of the thing, the right to the income from it, and the right to alienate it. The *extent* of these rights, however, is constrained by an injunction against waste. First and foremost, not wasting something means, simply, using it: where there is enough and as good left for others, no one will intentionally waste things, because it is not practical to do so. We use things because we need to, and any use would be less wasteful than no use. Some uses may benefit everyone; where some uses have positive effects on other persons, *those* uses are preferred because they are *relatively* less wasteful. Finally, when there is *not* enough and as good left for others, it would be wasteful, Locke thinks, to allow the conveniences of some to overbalance the needs of others. And insofar as the structure of property rights influences how things are used, limiting those rights may well result in less wasteful practices.

The structure of Locke's arguments leaves open the possibility that the extent and content of property rights justified under conditions of abundance are subject to subsequent modification under conditions of scarcity. However, Locke gives no clear indication of what the resultant bundle of rights might look like. In the next section, I explore how variations in resources' factor endowments affect how they can be used, and how, therefore, different bundles of rights might arise for different resources.

THE VARIABLE NATURE OF RESOURCES

As was discussed at the end of the last chapter, resources can be analyzed and compared with one another in terms of three factors: indivisibility, excludability, and jointness. Indivisibility refers to the degree to which a resource can be physically divided up or removed from the common pool; excludability refers to the degree to which access to the resource can be physically controlled; and jointness refers to the degree to which more than one person can make use of that resource. If more than one person can use a resource at the same time, then it exhibits simultaneous jointness; if it can be used more than once, either by the same person or by different persons, then it exhibits serial jointness. Accordingly, there are a series of questions I want to explore in this section. First, what degrees of these factors does Locke think are exhibited by the resources we use? Second, is he correct? And, third, if he were wrong, how would a corrected or expanded picture of resource factor endowments affect Locke's arguments about the extent and content of property rights?

Almost all resources can be used in a variety of different ways, and different uses of a particular resource may require different amounts of it. When a resource becomes scarce, it is reasonable to try to use that resource as judiciously as possible, which is to say that we should waste as little of it as possible. As I argued earlier, Locke's injunction against waste can be understood as a preference, all else being equal, for using things in ways consonant with the general good. If some particular use, or some particular way of using a resource, would enable more people to use it, then *that* use would be preferred to another that allowed fewer people to use the resource. In other words, when faced with scarcity, we should try to use a resource in a way that increases its overall degree of jointness. As we shall see, for some resources, not dividing them up and excluding others from using them may well increase their jointness.

Turning, then, to the first question, we have seen that for Locke, property rights in external goods arise from and are directed toward the productive use of those goods. He maintains that all such goods must first be marked off and removed from the commons "*before* they can be of any use, or at all beneficial to any particular Man."[61] So for Locke, a resource must first exhibit a low degree of indivisibility, or a high degree of divisibility, in order for any property rights in it to arise, because he believes that only such resources are capable of being used productively. We will need to say something more about the cogency of this position. For the moment, I only want to point out that for Locke any resource that is practicably indivisible—due, perhaps, to technical constraints or boundary indeterminacy—is immune from any sort of ownership. Thus, he views the world's vast oceans, what he calls "that great and still remaining Common of Mankind," as a resource lying beyond the purview of property-rights relationships.[62]

Not only must the resource be easily divisible in order for it to be used, but such division must, Locke thinks, afford the user *exclusive* use of it; when one uses a thing, he says, one thereby excludes the common right of others. As I discussed earlier, for Locke, it is not the mere act of dividing off or removing some thing from the commons that gives someone exclusive control over it. Rather, such exclusivity obtains only when what has been removed is subsequently *used*, or is intended to be used, by that individual. So, in order for me to have exclusive rights to what I have divided off or taken from the commons, I must be able to use *all* of it. One gets a strong sense that Locke thinks there is a close correlation between how much of a resource an individual needs or wants and how much of it he or she is readily able to divide off or remove from the commons. That is, he seems to take for granted that most resources could be divided up sufficiently close to what can be exclusively used by an individual. He certainly thinks that people have strong incentives to remove only what they really do need or want from the commons.[63] Moreover, his examples— apples, deer, land, and so on—tend to be of things that can be quite easily removed in usable quantities. That, I take it, is the reason he says that someone who intentionally takes more than he or she can use has done "a foolish thing," because there is simply no good reason for someone "to labour for more than he could make use of."[64] All this suggests that Locke takes the degree of divisibility and the degree of excludability of any particular resource to be more or less equivalent.

If a resource is divided off for exclusive use, for example, picking an apple, then only one person at a time uses it, and we could say that the apple fails to exhibit any degree of simultaneous jointness. If that exclusive use is a one-time affair, for example, eating the apple, then we could also say that the apple fails to exhibit any degree of serial jointness either. As we have already seen, Locke thinks that "[t]he greatest part of *things really useful* to the Life of Man ... *are* generally things of short duration; such as, if they are not consumed by use, will decay and perish of themselves."[65] It might be tempting, then, to conclude that Locke thinks most of the things we use fail to exhibit any jointness at all. But this is not entirely correct. Locke seems well aware that different individuals can use the same resource at different times. He goes on to consider how one person can remove an apple from the commons and then barter it away or sell it to someone else for the latter's consumption. In such a case, the resource obviously does exhibit *some* degree of serial jointness. But because Locke thinks that the useful life of most resources is of a very short duration, he must think that few of them really do exhibit serial jointness of any significant degree. The selling or bartering of an apple from one person to another cannot be sustained for any length of time for the simple reason that the apple will soon spoil. And, of course, once it is eaten or otherwise consumed, that is, once its capital is used up, then it cannot be used by anyone again.

So, Locke's view about the nature of the resources we use is this: (1) most of the really useful stuff available in the world must be removed from its original, common state before it can be used at all; (2) such division gives the remover exclusive rights over it; and (3) very few of the things removed for one's use can be subsequently used by others. Stated in terms of factor endowments, Locke's position is that most productive resources exhibit a high degree of both divisibility and excludability, but a very low degree of serial jointness. If we look carefully at various resources, however, we see that this position cannot be correct.

Looking first at Locke's position on divisibility, he seems to believe that an undivided resource is never of any use to anyone; *that*, after all, is why the original, useless commons *needs* to be divided up in the first place. And both division and use of a resource (or the intention of use) are required before an individual can establish any property rights over it. Therefore, it seems as if individuals cannot have any use rights over either an undivided or an indivisible resource. While there may not be any purely *indivisible* resources,[66] the idea that *undivided* resources are never of *any use* to anyone is wholly anachronistic. We have come to find, if only in this century, that there is significant, perhaps incalculable, value in leaving some resources, for example, an entire forest, undivided and undisturbed. Such resources are valuable—whether for supplying flora and fauna with habitat, renewing our tainted air and water, or refreshing our tired minds—precisely because they are undivided. We have, moreover, collectively decided to grant people *limited rights* to use such resources without thereby granting them more extensive rights. One has the right to go to places like a city park or a national forest and enjoy limited, personal use of them, but one has no right to sell, get income from, or use up the capital of those places. So, Locke's position that division and extensive use rights simply fall out of and are concomitant with one's need to use things is simply not true for all resources. Some resources can be used—and are clearly better used or even, perhaps, *only* usable at all—when they are kept more or less intact.

If we look at some resources, even one Locke himself uses as an example, we can see that their degrees of divisibility and excludability need not be the same. Locke, for instance, says that the law of reason "makes the Deer, that *Indian's* who hath killed it."[67] However, if all that the Indian intended to use was just a pound of venison or just the animal's hide, then, by Locke's own admission, the other parts of the animal would *not* be subject to the Indian's exclusive control, because exclusivity obtains only when what has been removed is intended to be *used* by that individual. It is true that one needs to divide off or remove a whole deer from the commons, that is, kill it, before one can use *any* of its meat or hide, but such removal does not itself give the remover claim-rights over *all* of the deer. Trees are another resource that comes readily to mind as being similar to deer in this respect: I have to cut down an entire tree to build a canoe, but I do not need the whole tree in order to build it. When there is no shortage of deer or trees, so that no one is materially disadvantaged by the wasting of a little meat, hide, or wood, then the why not? argument allows such waste: any use of a deer or a tree would be less wasteful than no use of it. When venison, or deer hide, or wood becomes scarce, however, such relative waste is unconscionable. In such situations, we might have good reasons for wanting to restrict the killing of deer or the cutting of trees unless all of their parts can be used, or for requiring hunters or tree cutters to sell, trade, or give away what they cannot use. Such restrictions and requirements would mean that more people could make use of a particular resource, thereby increasing that resource's jointness. Locke, in short, did not consider possible discrepancies between the divisibility and excludability of particular resources. Therefore, he did not recognize that such discrepancies might affect the extent and content of property rights when such resources become scarce.

As I said earlier, almost all resources can be used in a variety of different ways. A deer, for instance, can be used for either its meat or its hide. It can also be used for producing milk or as breeding stock for producing more deer. The main difference between the first two uses and the latter two is that whereas the first two require that the capital of the deer be used up, the latter two do not. If used for breeding or milk producing, the deer is usefully available to others in the future; if used for eating or clothing, it is not. Killing deer eliminates their serial jointness; breeding and milking them, however, maintains and even increases their productive capacity for others. If we consider a state of affairs where milk is in short supply, though meat and hide are readily available, we might then want to put restrictions on how deer are used. We might want to discourage their slaughter in favor of other uses that maintained or even increased their serial jointness— in essence using the benefit to others argument as a legitimate reply to the why not? argument. The one who captured a deer would still be recognized as having *some* rights over it, but the content and extent those rights might be somewhat restricted if doing so would be advantageous to others.

Contrary to what Locke thinks, then, some resources can be used without dividing them up or removing them from the common pool. Even where removal is required for use, it may not be possible to use all of what has been removed, that is, one who divides off some amount of a resource from the common pool may not be recognized as having exclusive use of all of it. And different uses can variously affect the serial jointness of a resource. In short, some resources exhibit *low* degrees of both divisibility and excludability, and a *high* degree of serial jointness. In such cases, more of the resource might be made available to everyone if an individual's use rights were restricted. A group of people who recognized this might, therefore, recognize only a more limited set of property rights. If one assumes, with Locke, that extensive private property rights are justified for highly divisible, exclusively usable resources that display little if any jointness, then it is not surprising that Locke fails to consider seriously any alternatives to private ownership. His entire account of property rights is informed by viewing external goods in a light that renders all of them as being similarly endowed. However, such a picture becomes much more colorful and full of possibilities once that monochromatic tint is removed.

I have argued that Locke operates with a rather hazy picture of the nature of resources. He thinks that undivided resources are useless; he thinks that division and exclusion are quite generally and naturally aligned for most resources; and he fails to consider either that many resources do exhibit jointness or that such jointness can be significantly affected by how a particular resource is used. Once we consider such matters in any detail, however, we see that such a picture fails to accurately portray the actual shape of the world in which we live. When a particular resource becomes scarce, so that not everyone is able to use it as they would like, then we should strive to waste as little of it as we can. We waste less, in at least one important sense of "waste," when we make more of that resource available for others to use. In situations where one person's use of a resource is both relatively wasteful and merely convenient, we may have good reasons, on Locke's view, for limiting that person's rights to use the resource, especially when doing so would increase the jointness of that resource and allow others with more pressing needs to have access to it as well.

The central point in all this is that because different resources have different factor endowments, different rights-arrangements may be in order for different resources. Cuzán, we should remember, makes two claims about water in the West. First, he maintains that water is just like any other resource, well suited to appropriation and exchange in a market economy. Second, he insists that Locke would have wholeheartedly endorsed this position. It is true that Locke gives us an account of how extensive ownership rights would naturally arise for resources. But that account, as we have seen, is based on assumptions about resources' factor endowments that are not notably prescient. The structure of Locke's arguments leaves room for maintaining that the rights applicable to one resource are not necessarily a good indication of the rights applicable to other resources because resources are *not* all alike in the way he imagines. The different factor endowments of various resources indicate different ways in which their jointness can be affected. It seems reasonable to maintain that the extent and content of property rights should be proportioned to the purposes or uses they serve, and that different purposes or uses may well support different bundles of rights.

Water in the West exhibits factor endowments significantly different from those Locke envisions. Eighty percent of the water diverted from the Colorado River, the major source of surface water in seven western states, is used for irrigating crops. Much of that water is simply absorbed into the soil, where it percolates through the ground and eventually flows back into the river, and downstream cultivators make subsequent use of it: "On rivers like the Colorado . . . the same water may be used *eighteen times* over."[68] On the two occasions when Locke does mention using water from a fountain or a river, he assumes that it exhibits no jointness whatsoever: it is removed only for drinking, so that the capital of the thing is used up.[69] However, much of the water used in the West is subsequently returned to the river and used again by others downstream. In other words, western water exhibits a *high* degree of serial jointness.

Because that water is often diverted long distances, much of it is lost through evaporation; this, when combined with seepage from diversion ditches and antiquated irrigation systems, means that much more water is often removed from the river than is actually put to use. That is, it is not easy to divide off from the river only that amount of water one needs; much of it is wasted before it is ever used. In this sense, western water exhibits a *low* degree of divisibility.

In addition to this, the dynamics of water use in the West means that one cultivator's use of water negatively impacts others. Evaporation makes the remaining water saltier; because salt formations are a ubiquitous feature of the Colorado River basin, the already salt-laden water must often travel through such formations on its way back to the river, "reaching saline levels thirty times higher than at the diversion point."[70] The cumulative effect of saltier water continuously being diverted again and again as it makes its way downstream has caused the salt content of the river to increase fourfold in the last fifty years.[71] Each cultivator's use degrades the quality of the water for others; in this sense, no use is exclusive to any one user, because each use impacts others. Western water, then, exhibits a *low* degree of excludability.

I have argued that Locke, had he thought more about certain features of resources, property rights, and their interrelationship, might indeed have found something objectionable about individuals having extensive private property rights over water in the West. In light of the factor endowments exhibited by that resource, we may have to go well beyond Locke's actual account of property in order to think coherently about property rights for water and other resources with similar factor endowments. There has been and continues to be a vibrant legal, economic, and political debate about how best to manage this now-scarce resource. There is room within the structure of Locke's arguments for limiting the extent and content of private property rights over resources if, by doing so, less of those resources will be wasted. Insofar as other rights-arrangements would indeed reduce waste and make more water available for westerners, Locke's account of property would support such alternative arrangements.

NOTES

1. See Lawrence C. Becker, *Property Rights: Philosophic Foundations* (London: Routledge and Kegan Paul, 1977), 48; Virginia Held, Introduction to *Property, Profits, and Economic Justice* (Belmont, WA: Wadsworth, 1980), 5–6; James O. Grunebaum, *Private Ownership* (London: Routledge and Kegan Paul, 1987), 66–67; Thomas Mautner, "Locke on Original Appropriation," *American Philosophical Quarterly* 19, no. 3 (July 1982): 267–268; and Jeremy Waldron, *The Right to Private Property* (Oxford: Clarendon, 1988), 259. General discussion of and replies to these criticisms are offered by A. John Simmons in both *The Lockean Theory of Rights* (Princeton, NJ: Princeton University Press, 1993), 235–236, and "Original-Acquisition Justifications of Private Property," *Social Philosophy and Policy* 11, no. 2 (Summer 1994), 75–78.

2. Alfred Z. Cuzán, "Appropriators versus Expropriators: The Political Economy of Water in the West," in *Water Rights: Scarce Resource Allocation, Bureaucracy, and the Environment*, ed. Terry L. Anderson (Cambridge, MA: Ballinger Publishing for the Pacific Institute for Public Policy Research, 1983), 14; see also Donald Worster, *Rivers of Empire: Water, Aridity, and the Growth of the American West* (New York: Random House, Pantheon Books, 1985; reprint, New York: Oxford University Press, 1992), 351–352.

3. Cuzán, "Appropriators versus Expropriators," 17.

4. Timothy D. Tregarthen, "Water in Colorado: Fear and Loathing in the Marketplace," in *Water Rights*, ed. Terry L. Anderson (Cambridge, MA: Ballinger Publishing for the Pacific Institute for Public Policy Research, 1983), 119.

5. See Jack Hirshleifer, James DeHaven, and Jerome Milliman, *Water Supply* (Chicago: University of Chicago Press, 1969); and Terry L. Anderson and P. J. Hill, "The Evolution of Property Rights: A Study of the American West," *Journal of Law and Economics* 18 (1975), 163–179.

6. John Locke, *Two Treatises of Government*, vol. 2, *Second Treatise*, ed. Peter Laslett (Cambridge: Cambridge University Press, 1988), sections 29 and 31.

7. See, for instance, J. P. Day, "Locke on Property," *Philosophical Quarterly* 16 (July 1966), 207; and Simmons, *Lockean Theory of Rights*, 228n.

8. Locke, *Two Treatises of Government*, 2:32, 33, 38, 45, 117, 120; see also Simmons, *Lockean Theory of Rights*, 311.

9. Locke, *Two Treatises of Government*, 2:33.

10. William Goldfarb, *Water Law*, 2d ed. (Chelsea, MI: Lewis, 1988), 33.

11. Worster, *Rivers of Empire*, 92; see also Donald J. Pisani, *Water, Land, and Law in the West* (Lawrence: University of Kansas Press, 1996), 12–17.

12. Tregarthen, "Water in Colorado," 119–120.

13. For a synopsis of such interpretations, see Simmons, *Lockean Theory of Rights*, 3–11.

14. Ibid., 11.

15. Locke, *Two Treatises of Government*, 2:26. The consequentialist reading of Locke's state of nature justification for private property rights is nowhere clearer. See Grunebaum, *Private Ownership*, 59–60.

16. A sufficient condition for the state of nature is the lack of a commonly agreed upon authority. See Locke, *Two Treatises of Government*, 2:19; see also Simmons, *Lockean Theory of Rights*, 17–18.

17. See Locke, *Two Treatises of Government*, 2:3, 38, 45, 50.

18. Ibid., 2:45.

19. For similar sentiments, see Alan Ryan, "Self-Ownership, Autonomy, and Property Rights," in *Property*, ed. J. Roland Pennock and John W. Chapman (New York: New York University Press, 1980), 243.

20. Locke, *Two Treatises of Government*, 2:25

21. We do not need God to reveal this to us: "The State of Nature has a law of nature to govern it, . . . And Reason . . . is that law." Locke, *Two Treatises of Government*, 2:6. "Reason tells us to preserve ourselves." Ibid., 2:16.

22. Locke, *Two Treatises of Government*, 2:25, 26; John Locke, *Two Treatises of Government*, vol. 1, *First Treatise*, ed. Peter Laslett (Cambridge: Cambridge University Press, 1988), section 40. Common ownership could be another situation where everything was common; that is, people could *consent* and *agree* to leave some resource common. Locke is aware of the distinction, and he makes it quite clear that positive communities, such as the English commons of his day, left "common by Compact," are to be contrasted with the initial state of the world, when things were "quite otherwise." Ibid., 2:35; see also 1:40, 2:28. A more detailed discussion can be found in Simmons, *Lockean Theory of Rights*, 236–243, 279–280.

23. Locke, *Two Treatises of Government*, 2:31; see also 2:33, 35.

24. See Becker, *Property Rights*, 28–30.

25. Locke, *Two Treatises of Government*, 2:37, emphasis added.

26. Ibid.; see also 2:41, 42.

27. Ibid., 2:6.

28. Ibid., 2:138.

29. The injunction against harm is a background condition for Locke. See Locke, *Two Treatises of Government*, 2:6; and Nozick, *Anarchy, State, and Utopia*, 171.

30. Locke, *Two Treatises of Government*, 2:27.

31. Ibid., 2:26.

32. Simmons, *Lockean Theory of Rights*, 273.

33. See especially David Hume, *A Treatise of Human Nature*, bk. 3, pt. 2., sec. 3. Ed. L. A. Selby-Bigge. Oxford: Clarendon, 1888), 505–506n; Grunebaum, *Private Ownership*, 55–59; Held, *Property, Profits, and Economic Justice*, 5–6; Mautner, "Locke on Original Appropriation," 267–268; and Nozick, *Anarchy, State, and Utopia*, 174–175.

34. It is primarily to counter the various objections to the mixing argument(s) that Simmons develops his account. See Simmons, *Lockean Theory of Rights*, 267–277.

35. Locke, *Two Treatises of Government*, 2:28.

36. Cuzán, "Appropriators versus Expropriators," 15, original emphasis.

37. Anderson and Hill, "Evolution of Property Rights," 176.

38. Locke, *Two Treatises of Government*, 2:19; see also A. John Simmons, *On the Edge of Anarchy* (Princeton, NJ: Princeton University Press, 1993), 17–18.

39. Locke, *Two Treatises of Government*, 2:14.

40. Ibid.

41. Lawrence C. Becker, "The Moral Basis of Property Rights," in *Property*, ed. J. Roland Pennock and John W. Chapman (New York: New York University Press, 1980), 205; see also Simmons, *Lockean Theory of Rights*, 223.

42. Locke, *Two Treatises of Government*, 2:28–30.

43. Ibid., 2:27, 31.

44. Richard A. Epstein, "On the Optimal Mix of Private and Common Property," in *Property Rights*, ed. Ellen Frankel Paul, Fred D. Miller Jr., and Jeffrey Paul (Cambridge: Cambridge University Press, 1994), 18.

45. Locke, *Two Treatises of Government*, 2:31; see also Mautner, "Locke on Original Appropriation," 260; Simmons, *Lockean Theory of Rights*, 282–283, 289; and Waldron, *Right to Private Property*, 321–322.

46. See Simmons, *Lockean Theory of Rights*, 229–230.

47. Locke, *Two Treatises of Government*, 2:37.

48. Ibid., 2:47.

49. If there was some external good that human action could not alter, for example, a meteor impervious to our attempts at modifying it, then the right to the capital of that thing, though *logically* entailed, would not be *materially* possible. I take it, however, that the logical possibility of modi-

fying things is included in the right to use those things. In such cases, we lack the power, but not the claim-right.

50. Locke, *Two Treatises of Government*, 1:92. We should take note of the qualification at the end of this quote; destruction is only justified for Locke when *need* requires it, and not when mere comfort or whimsy is the driving force. This restriction differs from the concept of full private ownership, where my rights over, for example, a desk, allow me to smash it to bits for whatever reason I care to consider, no matter how frivolous it may be. Locke's inclusion of this restriction allows us to conclude, along with Simmons, that "the right to freely destroy our property for whatever reason we choose may be a part of the liberal concept of 'full ownership,' but it is not a component of Lockean property." See Simmons, *Lockean Theory of Rights*, 233. Locke, then, is immune to charges that his account of property fails to yield the full rights of ownership, for he is not trying to defend such a view. For a criticism of Locke that runs along these lines, see Becker, *Property Rights*, 39–45.

51. Locke, *Two Treatises of Government*, 2:31, 37, 38.

52. Ibid., 2:46.

53. Ibid., 2:41.

54. Ibid., 2:38, emphasis added; see also 2:31, 37, 46.

55. This was the thinking of early advocates of western settlement. And since land in the West could not be cultivated without diverting water, broad and nearly absolute property rights over water were granted to settlers as well. See Pisani, *Water, Land, and Law in the West*, 14.

56. Locke, *Two Treatises of Government*, 2:30.

57. Totally frivolous destruction involves labor costs but *no* benefits, and is, therefore, the most nonpragmatic and wasteful of activities.

58. Locke, *Two Treatises of Government*, 2:26; 2:6.

59. Ibid., 2:183; see also Simmons, *Lockean Theory of Rights*, 49–51. Although Locke says this in the middle of discussion about conquest, the generality of the statement suggests that he meant it to apply to other situations as well. He says elsewhere that the purpose of the natural law is "the general Good of those under that Law" (2:57), and that when a "nobler use" of a resource calls for negatively impacting others, we may do so (2:6). As a general rule, it would be nobler or better if resources were used to the "preservation of the whole" (2:171) if by doing so we would interfere only with the conveniences of some.

60. Ibid., 2:134, 171.

61. Ibid., 2:26, emphasis added.

62. Ibid., 2:30.

63. Ibid., 2:31, 36, 37, 48.

64. Ibid., 2:46, 51.

65. Ibid., 2:46.

66. We should not, I think, criticize Locke for failing to foresee a time when even the oceans could be divided up among nations; we ourselves

should not discount the possibility that, someday, the moon or even whole sectors of outer space could be usefully divided up.

67. Locke, *Two Treatises of Government*, 2:30.

68. Mark Reisner, *Cadillac Desert: The American West and Its Disappearing Water* (New York: Penguin, 1993), 459.

69. See Locke, *Two Treatises of Government*, 2:29, 33.

70. Reisner, *Cadillac Desert*, 460.

71. See Norris Hundley Jr., *Water and the West: The Colorado River Compact and the Politics of Water in the American West* (Berkeley: University of California Press, 1975), 315; and Worster, *Rivers of Empire*, 320–322.

5

Economics and Property Rights

Much of the confusion in environmental policy stems from a fundamental misunderstanding of possible resource regimes. The "tragedy of the commons" allegory arising from the writings of Garrett Hardin has done much to confuse scholars and others, and hence meaningful progress in understanding resource management has been stifled.

Daniel W. Bromley, *Environment and Economy*

The *purely* economic man is indeed close to being a social moron. Economic theory has been much preoccupied with this rational fool decked in the glory of his *one* all-purpose preference ordering. To make room for the different concepts related to his behavior we need a more elaborate structure.

Amartya K. Sen, "Rational Fools"

INTRODUCTION

Over the last two chapters, we have seen that political philosophers, at least within the liberal political tradition, have focused on private-property solutions to resource-scarcity problems, tending either to misrepresent common-property arrangements or to ignore them altogether. Neoclassical economists have been similarly focused. In their view, private property wins out over all other forms of property, particularly common property, because when individuals have extensive private property rights, they are able to make the best, or the most efficient, use of resources. As economists Terry L. Anderson and P. J. Hill put it, "In the final analysis it is the degree of private property rights that determines efficient resource allocation."[1]

The cogency of this view, however, is open to challenge because it relies heavily on three assumptions that, when examined carefully, prove to warrant our deep suspicion. I maintain that because these assumptions are unreliable, the argument that private property will work better than a common-property arrangement for a resource like water in the West is unsound.

First, many economists operate with a confused picture of what a common-property arrangement actually looks like, something that was touched on briefly in chapter 3, and that is discussed again in this chapter. The tendency among economists has been to see *any* state of affairs where resources are being used by a group of people in common as a *no-property* situation.[2] And, I argue, this conflation of common property with what I will call a limited-user open-access situation has often led economists to mischaracterize common-property arrangements as the primary *cause* of a resource's depletion and degradation. However, armed with the picture of common-property arrangements that was developed in chapter 3, we can see that this need not be true. To paraphrase one Nobel Laureate in economics: Not being overly clear about what a common-property arrangement looked like, the view that such arrangements simply could not work was never clearly wrong.[3]

Second, most economists have focused on only one set of problems, those arising from analogues of the multiplayer nonzero-sum game known as the Prisoner's Dilemma.[4] As we will see, each player in a Prisoner's Dilemma game has an incentive to act in ways that, in the end, turn out to be detrimental to *every* player. There are two crucial assumptions in such games: (1) each player decides what to do regardless of what others might decide, and (2) each player is motivated only by narrow self-interest. However, this austere model of behavior fails to represent adequately how human beings actually can and do interact with one another. As Amartya K. Sen suggests in the second quote that opens this chapter, there is room within economic analysis for a more elaborate structure. We do not always decide what to do in isolation from and irrespective of others' decisions: we communicate, negotiate, bargain, generate mutual expectations, and so on. And more importantly, we do not always act in ways motivated only by narrow self-interest: we recognize and act from commitments, duties, and so on to one another that go beyond mere self-interest. In short, economists tend to operate with an overly simplistic picture of how individuals interact with one another, and this tendency has resulted in an unnecessarily limited view of how resource depletion can be combated. In the final chapter, I sketch a constructive account of a more elaborate structure of human behavior, one within which a common-property arrangement need not succumb to "the tragedy of the commons." Here, I am concerned with elaborating the economic model within which such tragedies are seen as being difficult to avert without giving people private property rights over common resources.

Third, economists have tended to operate with a rather monochromatic picture of resources' factor endowments. Since the publication of Garrett Hardin's highly influential article of the same title, "the tragedy of the commons" has become a catch-all phrase among economists and others concerned with the overexploitation of resources susceptible to joint use. The main example Hardin uses—herders grazing their cattle upon an open, common rangeland—is taken by many economists to be an accurate model of *all* commons problems. However, there are certain resources that exhibit factor endowments that are not captured by Hardin's scenario; the presence of those factor endowments tells against private-property arrangements for those resources. In other words, because economists have rushed to explain with a single, attractive metaphor a whole range of problems associated with common resources, they have "obscured some important distinctions in the physical characteristics and the manner of use of [those resources]."[5] Certain characteristics of resources may make those resources less amenable to private-property arrangements. In such cases, a common-property arrangement may be more effective for dealing with resource scarcity.

I will use Hardin's account of "the tragedy of the commons" as a starting point for discussing the issues sketched earlier. In the course of this discussion, we will have to grapple with some key economic concepts, the most important of these being externalities. As will become clear, certain resources exhibit externalities for which private property is not well suited. Armed with both a more accurate picture of common property and a more elaborate structure of individuals' behavior, a common-property arrangement emerges as a viable alternative to private ownership for such resources. Water in the West is one of those resources. In the final chapter, I lay out an alternative to the Prisoner's Dilemma model of human behavior; I describe there the conditions under which the Assurance Game model becomes operative, and I show how those conditions either already exist or might be created in the American West.

THE TRAGEDY OF THE COMMONS

Hardin, in his now-famous 1968 article entitled "The Tragedy of the Commons," asks us to imagine a common pasture available for everyone to use.[6] This pasture is used exclusively for grazing cattle. The cattle themselves are owned by individual herders, who graze their cattle in order to sell them in the marketplace. Each herder, it is assumed, will graze as many cattle as he or she profitably can on the pasture. And as long as the carrying capacity of the pasture is not reached, that is, as long as the pasture is not overgrazed, this arrangement will not be a problem; Hardin envisions such an arrangement working reasonably well for centuries.[7] But, the time may well come when the pasture's carrying capacity has been reached, so that, when one more head of cattle is put there to graze, the pasture's ability to sustain both itself and that number of cattle cannot continue indefinitely. If the number of cattle is not reduced back to a level within the pasture's carrying capacity, both the pasture and the cattle themselves will begin to deteriorate.

If we assume that every herder knows this to be the situation, the crucial question to ask is: If left to his or her own devices, what will each herder decide to do? Hardin's answer is this:

As a rational being, each herdsman seeks to maximize his gain. Explicitly or implicitly, more or less consciously, he asks, "What is the utility *to me* of adding one more animal to my herd?" This utility has one negative and one positive component.

1. The positive component is a function of the increment of one animal. Since the herdsman receives all the proceeds from the sale of the additional animal, the positive utility is nearly +1.

2. The negative component is a function of the additional overgrazing created by one more animal. Since, however, the effects of overgrazing are shared by all the herdsmen, the negative utility for any particular decision-making herdsman is only a fraction of -1.

Adding together the component partial utilities, the rational herdsman concludes that the only sensible course for him to pursue is to add another animal to his herd. And another. . . . But this is the conclusion reached by each and every rational herdsman sharing a commons.[8]

This example is elaborated and analyzed later in this chapter. Here, the main thing to notice is that the situation Hardin describes is *not* a common-property arrangement. As he describes it, the resource, the pasture, is open for *anyone* to use. As was discussed in chapter 3, one necessary feature of a common-property arrangement is that in it, only a *limited set* of individuals is allowed to use the resource. The concept of a common-property arrangement, "implies that potential resource users who are not members of a group [of owners] are excluded" from using the resource.[9] It might be argued that the "everyone" Hardin uses is meant to refer, implicitly, to the limited and determinable members of some identifiable community. In that case, the number of (potential) users would be limited to those in what I call the resource community. But even if this were true, we would *still* not have a common-property arrangement. Limited group size, while necessary, is not a sufficient condition for a common-property arrangement. As was also discussed in chapter 3, the other necessary condition for a common-property arrangement is that the members of the resource community must have established clearly defined property rights among themselves.[10] In Hardin's example, however, the herders who are using the pasture have made no attempt either to limit their joint uses or to ensure that everyone adheres to such limits.

In fact, Hardin has not described a *property* arrangement at all. He has, rather, described an *open-access* situation, where everyone (in the community) has liberties to use the resource and no one (in the community) has any duties to refrain from using it. What he describes is not a tragedy of common *property*; rather, it is a tragedy of *open access*—or, as will be clarified, a tragedy of *limited-user* open access. What is most tragic of all, however, is that it is not clear that Hardin even recognizes a distinction between common property and open access. When he goes on to discuss how the tragedy of the commons can be avoided, he mentions private ownership and state ownership as possible solutions, but common-property arrangements, as I have described them, are not even considered.[11] It is not only that he calls a "commons" what is more accurately labeled an "open-access resource," but it is also that his doing so results in common-property arrangements being overlooked altogether.

Hardin is not alone in failing to differentiate a common-property arrangement from a situation of open access; other economists have also made the same mistake. Douglas North and Robert P. Thomas, in a well-respected paper on economic history, describe the economic state of traditional societies as one in which resources "were initially held as common property. This type of property right implies free access by all to the resource."[12] Harold Demsetz, in one of the now-classic articles on the rise of property institutions, describes what he labels "communal ownership" as a situation where there is "a right which can be exercised by all. . . . Communal property rights allow anyone to use the land."[13] What North and Thomas describe is clearly a no-property situation; and Demsetz, despite his use of the terms "rights" and "ownership," describes not a common-property arrangement, but rather an open-access resource. Such instances lend support to Glenn G. Stevenson's assertion that "we look about us and everywhere find resources being used by a group of people in common and are tempted to say, 'Aha! Here is another "tragedy of the commons.' "[14]

As with Hardin, Demsetz's mischaracterization of open access as a case of communal ownership causes him to reject both arrangements in the same breath. As we will see in the following sections, the main economic problem in the type of situation Hardin describes is that some of the costs of an individual's actions are not borne by that individual, and hence those costs constitute *social costs*, or externalities. "The great disadvantage of communal property," writes Demsetz, is that it "results in great externalities."[15] In his subsequent discussion about ways to eliminate such externalities, he almost exclusively discusses private ownership—ignoring *state* ownership altogether—and, in effect, recognizes only a dichotomy of ownership systems: private ownership and open access.[16] By conflating communal property with open access, Demsetz, in effect, saddles both with the same problem, namely, externalities.

Failing to differentiate common property from open access is not simply a matter of semantic conflation. Such conflation has caused theorists like Hardin, Demsetz, and others either to dismiss out of hand or to ignore altogether another possible *property* arrangement that is substantially different from the *no-property* situation with which they have associated it. For clarity's sake, then, we should understand "open access" as any state of affairs where (1) a resource is susceptible to use by multiple individuals, and (2) where no attempt has been made at self-management among those users. Where no group of users or resource community has been identified, then we have the classic unlimited-user open-access situation, where there are no restrictions either on who can use the resource or on how it can be used. This state of affairs would be equivalent to John Locke's state of nature. Where a group or resource community *has* been identified, but where no use restrictions have been implemented, then we have a situation of limited-user open access.[17] It is this latter situation that I will take Hardin to be describing.

Empirical work over the last twenty-five years has shown that there exists in the world a wide-ranging assortment of successful common-property arrangements. By successful, it is meant that the resource "has not been squandered, that some level of investment in the [resource] has occurred, and that the co-owners of the resource are not in a perpetual state of anarchy."[18] The grazing commons of Switzerland, the marine coastal fisheries of Turkey, and various irrigation schemes around the world—including irrigation districts in the American West—have all been cited as examples of successful common-property arrangements.[19] What makes these and other examples instances of common-property arrangements is that a well-delineated group of individuals, what I call a resource community, manages the resource according to "explicitly or implicitly understood rules about who may take how much of the resource."[20] When the rules of use are both explicit and enforceable, they amount to a system of property rights. So, not every successful system of property or ownership needs to look like private property. The fact that common-property arrangements are alive and well in the world suggests that such an arrangement cannot be dismissed out of hand.

As we shall see in the next section, the "tragedy of the commons" operates as an analog to the Prisoner's Dilemma. Since Hardin's discussion is most commonly and profitably taken to be an example of such a dilemma,[21] we need to be clear about precisely which type of property arrangement is under attack in such analyses. It is *not* a common-property arrangement; rather, it is a situation of limited-user open access, which is not a property situation at all.

LIMITED-USER OPEN ACCESS AND THE PRISONER'S DILEMMA

It will be helpful if we make some modifications and clarifications to Hardin's example. First, let us simplify it and stipulate that there are just two herders, Barney and Fred, and that they each originally own fifty cattle.[22] The stipulation that each originally owns the same number of cattle is meant to model a situation of economic parity between the two individuals. In Prisoner's Dilemma games, all the parties, or players, are typically modeled as having equal payoff tables. And when bargaining is introduced into the picture, as will be done later on, a parity situation eliminates possible bargaining-power discrepancies.

We are at the point in the story where the pasture has reached its carrying capacity, meaning that the addition of one more head of cattle to it will be detrimental to both the pasture and the cattle. Among other things, each animal will be able to eat slightly less than it could before, and, consequentially, each animal will fetch a slightly lower price in the marketplace. To put some numbers on all of this: Assume that the carrying capacity of the pasture is one hundred cattle, and that at or below this number of cattle, each animal is worth $100. However, when the 101st animal is added to the pasture, each animal is then worth only $99; when the 102nd animal is added, each animal is then worth only $98; and so on.[23] Barney and Fred are both well aware of all this, and each now has a choice to make: either to add another animal to the pasture or to refrain from doing so; this latter option will be called stinting.[24]

There are two crucial assumptions in this scenario, just as there were in Hardin's original example. First, both Barney and Fred seek only to maximize their own expected individual gains (or to minimize their own expected individual losses).[25] Second, no discussion, collusion, or negotiation has been attempted, that is, Barney and Fred have not tried to establish any rules to coordinate their use of the pasture. As we shall see, and as we should expect to see, the solution to commons problems relies on some kind of rules being agreed to (and followed) by the members of the resource community. But given the stipulated conditions that each is to reason alone only about what is in his own best interest, let us consider the situation in some detail.

From Barney's perspective, if both he and Fred choose to stint, neither of them will make any gains nor incur any losses. If Barney unilaterally chooses to add another animal to his herd, he will lose $50 because the value of each of his original animals will be reduced by $1 (this is the negative component in Hardin's discussion), but he will receive $99 for selling the additional animal (this is the positive component), thus he will realize a net gain of $49.[26] If Barney chooses to stint, but Fred chooses to add another animal, then Barney will lose $50, unless he too then immediately adds another animal himself. By adding another animal after Fred has done so, Barney will make less money than he made originally—$4,998 versus $5,000—but he will minimize his losses—$2 versus $50. So, no matter what Fred does, whether he decides to stint or to add another animal to his herd, it is in Barney's best interest to add another animal anyway, and another one after that, until it is no longer in his best interest to do so.

Of course, things look exactly the same from Fred's point of view, too. And adding more herders to the picture does nothing to change the overall picture. As long as any herder either receives more benefits or incurs fewer losses by adding another animal to his or her herd, then there is an incentive for that herder to do so.[27] And, as Hardin writes: "Therein is the tragedy. Each man is locked into a system that compels him to increase his herd without limit—in a world that is limited. Ruin is the destination toward which all men rush, each pursuing his own best interest in a society that believes in the freedom of the commons. Freedom in a commons brings ruin to all."[28]

From the point of view of the society or community as a whole, which in this case is just Barney and Fred, it is better, overall, if both of them choose to stint. At its carrying capacity, the total income produced by the pasture is $10,000. Above that level of grazing, we can see that the overall income produced by the pasture steadily decreases: it is only $9,999 with 101 animals being grazed, $9,996 with 102, and so on. The next-best result would be realized if one of the herders stinted and the other did not; this would make one herder better off and the other one worse off. Where Barney and Fred are each grazing fifty animals at the pasture's carrying capacity, if Barney then adds one more animal, his income will be $5,049, and Fred's will fall to $4,950. And the worst situation, either from the point of view of the whole community or from the point of view of either of its members, would be if Barney and Fred both decided to add another animal. If Barney and Fred both add another animal, then each will receive only $4,998; if they both add two more animals, then they each will receive only $4,992; and so on. And this, tragically, is exactly what the logic of the situation tells us will happen.

This situation corresponds to the Prisoner's Dilemma or, as it is sometimes called, the "isolation paradox."[29] The paradox here is that although any player P would prefer an outcome where either everyone chooses to stint or everyone but P chooses to stint, no one, in fact, actually does choose to stint. The strategy of adding another animal is said to be "strictly dominant" because it is followed regardless of any one individual's expectations of other individuals' behavior. As Sen describes it, "Irrespective of each person's expectations of others' actions, each person prefers to [add another animal], i.e., the strategy of [adding another animal] strictly dominates over the alternative."[30] That is, no matter what *anyone* or *everyone else* does, there will still be an incentive for *me* to act in a way that ends up being detrimental to *all of us*. And what seems rational for me seems rational for everyone else too. Acting alone—because, we should remember, it is assumed here that we cannot communicate, much less negotiate, about stinting—and acting solely from motives of narrow self-interest, the inevitable outcome is the one least desirable from either anyone's or everyone's point of view.

SOCIAL COSTS, NEGATIVE EXTERNALITIES, AND POLLUTION

The locus of the problem in the case of herders grazing their cattle upon a limited-user open-access pasture is that one individual receives the whole positive component, but that same individual suffers *only a portion* of the negative component. Barney, for instance, receives all the benefits or positive effects from unilaterally deciding to add another animal to his herd, but the costs, or negative effects, of overgrazing are shared by all the herders. If it is just Barney and Fred, and if each have a herd of fifty cattle, the *private costs* to Barney of adding one more animal to his herd is $50, which reflects the $1 reduction in the value of each of his other fifty animals. But the *total costs* incurred are $100, because the value of Fred's herd is similarly reduced. This difference between the private costs, those borne by Barney, and the total costs, those borne by everyone, represents the *social costs* of Barney's decision to add another animal. Social costs, as the economist Daniel W. Bromley describes them, are those costs "falling beyond the boundary of the decision-making unit that is responsible for [them]. This notion of costs going *beyond* the decision unit that creates them explains the origin of the term *externalities*."[31] It is the existence of externalities that constitutes the main economic problem with limited-user open-access situations.

To be more precise, it is the problem of *negative* externalities with which I am concerned, for we should notice in passing that externalities can be either positive or negative. What Bromley describes is more properly labeled a *negative* externality. Conversely, a *positive* externality can be thought of as a social *benefit*, or good, that extends beyond the person or decision-making unit responsible for creating it. If Fred and Barney are each now grazing fifty-one animals, and if, for example, Fred were to unilaterally decide to *remove* one of his animals, then that decision would produce a net social benefit of $3 ($9,999 versus $9,996), and we could consider it a positive externality.[32] National parks, roads, weather reports, and national defense are all typically used examples of resources that exhibit positive externalities: Individuals benefit from such things even though they themselves may not have (fully) borne the costs of creating and maintaining them. The effective management of such resources is sometimes discussed under the rubric of public goods problems.[33] It is with such goods that we typically encounter discussions of the free-rider problem, though as we shall see, individuals who create negative externalities can be said to be free riding as well. Most of the following distinctions made about different sorts of negative externalities can be applied to discussions of public goods problems as well. In what follows, however, the focus is on negative externalities. For parsimony's sake then, I will for the most part drop the modifier "negative," and it can be assumed that I am discussing *negative* externalities unless otherwise noted.

A key feature of externalities is that unwanted costs are *forced* upon one or several decision-making units by the unilateral actions of one or several other decision-making units. Issues of fairness aside, however, the existence of unwanted costs alone does not necessarily signal the existence of an economic problem in need of a solution. If, for example, a large retail chain decides to open a new store in a small town, thereby "forcing" the local merchants to lower their prices if they want to stay in business, the local merchants will no doubt consider themselves to have suffered unwanted costs from the retail chain's decision. From another point of view, however, the situation simply reflects the costs of doing business; and if the total benefits to the community increase because of the lowered prices, the community may well applaud the new retailer's decision to open up shop there. The community's other members more than welcome what is unwanted by the local merchants. More generally, what we have in this case is a so-called *pecuniary* externality, one that results from economic competition and is transmitted through the price system.[34] As long as the *total social benefits exceed the total social costs*, or as long as the market operates with allocative efficiency, it is not obviously clear that there are problems with such pecuniary externalities.[35] (As we shall see, however, some pecuniary externalities may be less benign than this one example suggests.)

What is of central interest here, and what captures the interest of economists concerned with natural resources, is the class of so-called *technological* externalities, those *nonprice-transmitted*, physical depletions of a resource that serve to erode others' ability to utilize it.[36] Barney's decision to add another animal above the pasture's carrying capacity produces just such an externality; the addition results in, inter alia, degradation to the pasture, which produces *net social costs* that are neither transmitted to Barney nor reflected in his utility calculus. Once the 101st animal is added, there is *not* enough and as good of the pasture left for everyone else. In terminology we have used earlier, we could say that the pasture's degree of *jointness*, the degree to which more than one person can make use of that resource, is reduced by Barney's action. If there were fewer than one hundred animals, Barney's addition of another animal would not affect the resource's jointness: At any grazing level below the pasture's carrying capacity, there is, for all intents and purposes, enough and as good of the resource left for others to use. In other words, the existence of technological externalities is one sign of a resource's scarcity.

It is not much of a stretch to say that the technological externalities in Hardin's example constitute a form of *pollution*, just as smoke from a factory, or chemicals, sewage, salt, and so on dumped into a river are forms of pollution. In each case, one decision-making unit's action in some sense spoils the resource for others, because the resource is no longer able to sustain itself and cannot be used to everyone's satisfaction. One small factory emitting smoke in an otherwise bucolic landscape, or one person dumping his or her bodily waste into a huge lake, does not necessarily constitute pollution because, at those use levels, the smoke or sewage will, presumably, dissipate and cause no palpable harm to anyone. Rather, pollution only occurs when the resource in question (the air, the water, or the pasture) can no longer absorb such uses without widespread or long-term (negative) effects to others, that is, when the resource becomes scarce.[37] We normally think of "pollution" in cases where something is *added* to a resource: smoke is released into the atmosphere, sewage is dumped into the water, or cattle are added to a pasture. But we could also label as "pollution" such actions as overfishing: for example, when too many bass have been *taken out* of a lake, the species can no longer sustain itself because of reduced reproduction rates. In fact, overgrazing could be considered a "taking out" as well: it is because too much grass is eaten that the pasture becomes degraded. In any case, whether from putting too much of something into or from taking too much of something out of a resource, "polluting" constitutes using a resource beyond the level where enough and as good of it is left for everyone else in the resource community to use.[38]

It is important to see, however, that pollution need not always be thought of as a technological externality; sometimes it is better thought of as a result of a pecuniary externality. That is, sometimes the emission of harmful smoke, the dumping of raw sewage, or overgrazing and overfishing are the result of a conscious trade-off, occurring as a result of the inexorable workings of the free market. While we may bemoan the degradation such actions cause, we can and do sometimes (at least try to) justify them in purely economic terms if, for example, the long-term and wide-spread social benefits are thought to outweigh the immediate costs of losing rivers, habitats, species, and so on. What I am suggesting is that the pollution that occurs as the conscious result of bargaining in the marketplace *is* transmitted through the price system, and is *not*, therefore, a technological externality. As long as all the costs of the decision to pollute are fully accounted for and taken into consideration, it takes some argument to show that, on purely *economic* grounds, there is indeed a problem in need of a solution. In other words, the mere act of polluting is not at issue here. Rather, what I am concerned with, and what I think most economists interested in such matters are concerned with as well, is situations where the decision whether to pollute or not is reached *without* taking into consideration *all* the relevant costs or all the relevant *benefits*. Polluting sometimes occurs because, after all the costs and benefits have been tallied up, it is considered profitable to do so. However, in *all* cases of technological externalities, some costs and benefits are not taken into account.[39] Another way to characterize the distinction is this: For economists, "pollution" is a neutral, descriptive term, whereas "technological externality" is a normative and derisive one. When an economist sees pollution, she may or may not see it as a problem in need of a solution; when she sees a technological externality, she *always* thinks that a solution needs to be found.

The problems associated with technological externalities can be thought of, then, as the problems arising from *some* instances of pollution, as it variously appears in its many guises. Technological externalities constitute a subclass of pollution problems. In limited-user open-access situations, such as that modeled in Hardin's analog of the Prisoner's Dilemma, polluting, if you will, becomes the strictly dominant strategy, because at least some of the costs of polluting are borne, in whole or in part, by others who also use the resource.

RECIPROCAL VERSUS NONRECIPROCAL EXTERNALITIES

We need to make one more distinction at this point, that between *reciprocal* and *nonreciprocal* externalities. A reciprocal externality occurs in situations where *each* user of the resource imposes negative externalities of like kind upon each other.[40] The case of Barney and Fred is an example of a reciprocal externality: Once the technical externalities of overgrazing manifest themselves, each new animal introduced into the pasture *affects all the other herders alike*.[41] A significant feature here is that the pasture admits of only one use, namely, grazing cattle. Reciprocal externalities most often occur in such cases, where all the users of a resource use it in the same way.[42] Most resources, however, actually admit of multiple uses. And among different uses, some affect a resource's jointness more than others do. This suggests that most resources that suffer from technological externality problems are plagued by the nonreciprocal variety.

As distinguished from a reciprocal externality, a *nonreciprocal* externality occurs when *some*, but not all, users of a resource produce externalities, and the externalities are *not* borne in kind by everyone in the resource community. Consider a river whose waters are used by, among other decision-making units, a paper mill M and a downstream farmer F. M produces a negative externality in the form of pulp, which causes stunted growth in F's corn. F's use of the water does not impact M's use, though F's use does impact downstream farmers by increasing the river's salinity, pesticide levels, and so on. Upstream farmers, other mills along the river, and all others whose uses of the water are unaffected by pulp, salt, and pesticides in the water do not experience either F's or M's action as an externality. This is clearly a case of a nonreciprocal externality, and it is precisely the sort of situation with which we are concerned.[43]

It is important to see that Hardin's example and, more generally, limited-user open-access situations that are analogues of the Prisoner's Dilemma, model reciprocal situations, where each member of the resource community imparts negative externalities on all other users. The literature on open-access resources has tended to focus on such situations.[44] And as we shall see, this tendency to discuss only reciprocal externalities has tended to make it look as if giving individuals private ownership of the resource will be a successful solution for *all* technological externality problems. But since not all technological externalities are reciprocal, the conclusion that private property is the preferred solution for all instances of technical externalities is arrived at too quickly.

FREE RIDING (OR FOUL DEALING)

Let us drop the assumption that the herders cannot communicate with one another, keeping in place the assumption that they are still motivated to act only from narrow self-interest. There is an incentive for everyone to agree to stint in such situations, for example, agree to graze only so many animals as the pasture can sustain without suffering degradation. We saw this earlier. But as we also saw that there is also a *greater* incentive for such agreements to be subsequently *broken*, because each herder would prefer it if every *other* herder stinted *but not himself*. This is the essence of the *free-rider problem*: "Even if an agreement is struck that specifies that all will refrain from further grazing, the strict dominance of the free-rider strategy makes such a contract unstable."[45]

As was discussed earlier, to say that some strategy is strictly dominant means that it is carried out regardless of any one individual's expectations of other individuals' behavior. Suppose every herder agrees to stint. From each and every particular herder's point of view, if everyone *else* can be expected to live by the agreement, then he himself can gain more by cheating. And if everyone else *does* cheat, then each and every herder must cheat too in order to minimize his losses, because the externalities produced by overgrazing are reciprocal. Regardless of my expectations of others' behavior then, whether I expect them to stint or to cheat, I expect to gain more (or to lose less) by adding another animal to my herd. Hence the instability of the agreement; each can be expected to cheat, or free ride, and unless stability is achieved, both the resource and the resource community can be expected to deteriorate.

So, the essence of the problem in Prisoner's Dilemma situations is not simply that the players cannot communicate. Rather, at its core is the problem that even if they are able to strike an agreement about cooperative behavior, there is still an overriding incentive for every player to subsequently break that agreement because each expects to receive more (or to lose less), in the short run at least, by cheating than by cooperating: the incentive structure is such that it does not matter which strategy, cooperating or stinting, the other player(s) may choose. The strict dominance of free-riding, or foul-dealing, behavior ensures an inferior outcome; everyone overgrazes.

EXTERNALITIES AND PRIVATE OWNERSHIP

Within neoclassical economics, the general solution to free-rider problems involves transforming the social costs of an individual's action into private costs via the establishment of enforceable property rights.[46] Whether it be by establishing a private property regime, or by establishing some other form of ownership, the idea is that those who produce externalities should be forced to take into account all the costs of their actions. The goal is to make individual decision-making units responsible for all the effects of their actions: if the benefits of an action outweigh all the costs, then the activity (e.g., overgrazing, emitting chemicals, or increasing salinity) will occur; if not, then individuals will refrain from such activities. If enforceable rights and duties can be established that correspond to these benefits and costs, then what has happened, in effect, is that externality has become internalized. As Demsetz writes, "The main allocative function of property rights is the internalization of beneficial and harmful effects."[47]

Given the incentive structure all players are expected to follow in Prisoner's Dilemmas or limited-user open-access situations, the implication to most economists has been that individuals should be given extensive private property rights, or private ownership, over the resource in question. In the most general sense, rights and their opposites, duties, specify how individuals may be benefited and harmed. As was discussed in chapter 3, the four types of Hohfeldian rights or right-surrogates (claim-rights, liberties, powers, and immunities) can all be considered advantages or benefits to those who have them; their respective opposites (duties, no-rights, liabilities, and disabilities) can all be considered disadvantages or losses by those who are so constrained. In economic terms, a property right can be thought of as "a claim to a benefit stream that [is protected] through the assignment of duty to others who may covet, or somehow interfere with, the benefit stream."[48] If I have a protected, exclusive claim-right to use some portion of a resource, then there is a concomitant duty incumbent on everyone else not to use that same portion of the resource. The security of my continued use constitutes a palpable benefit for me, and the loss of others' opportunity to interfere with that benefit stream through their own beneficial use constitutes a real cost to them. But where everyone has claim-rights, everyone has concomitant duties as well: Once exclusive property rights have been established for a particular resource, each member of the resource community now has a duty not to interfere with others' use of their portion of the benefit stream of the resource, and that duty constitutes an opportunity cost to each individual.

This suggests that in situations where the simultaneous assignment of rights and duties amounts to a *reciprocal trade-off*, private property rights might be an effective means for internalizing externalities. If the assignment of the advantages or benefits of rights to one individual or member of the resource community balances with the concomitant disadvantages or costs (i.e., harms) of duties assigned to others, then that is a strong basis indeed upon which interested individuals can reach an agreement about prudent resource use. If the resource in question is easily divisible into useful parcels, and if such division allows individuals to thereby insulate or exclude themselves from the deleterious effects of others' actions, then free riding can be combated effectively through the vesting of extensive private property rights.[49] This should be expected, given earlier discussions about the relationship between a resource's factor endowments and possible property-rights arrangements: jointly used resources that exhibit a high degree of both divisibility and excludability are especially amenable to private-property arrangements.[50] Fred, who now, let us say, has been granted private ownership of some portion of the pasture, may decide to build a fence around his private land. Doing so, let us assume, will not only keep Barney's cattle off Fred's land, but will also keep the effects of Barney's decision to overgraze off of Fred's land too: his animals and his land will not now deteriorate if Barney decides to add another animal.[51] Similarly, and just as importantly, the fence will keep all of Fred's cattle on his own land, and should he decide to add another animal to his herd, all the effects of overgrazing would be kept there as well. If those effects are now concentrated on, for example, half the pasture, we can (conservatively) estimate that the costs to Fred will be double what they were before, and that he will now decide not to add another animal to his herd.[52]

However, for some resource/use combinations, though dividing up the resource may be easy enough, dividing it up such that the deleterious effects of one decision-making unit's use of the resource does not spill over to injure other users is not so easily accomplished. For example, one cannot just build a fence and thereby stop airborne pollution, whether it is an industrial by-product or an agricultural insecticide, from wafting across the sky. Nor, as we saw in chapters 1 and 2, does giving people the right to use only a certain quantity of water from the Colorado River mean that the effects of that use, for example, increased salinity, will be borne wholly by that individual. More generally, where divisibility of the resource and excludability from the negative externalities of joint resource use diverge, giving individuals extensive private property rights over some portion of the resource may not cause the intended modifications in overall use patterns.

Furthermore, where the externalities of resource use are of a *nonreciprocal* nature, the very establishment of property rights within the resource community might be quite difficult. As was discussed earlier, the establishment of property rights where none currently exist amounts to agreeing to a trade-off: each party expects to receive both a benefit and a cost, and that is the basis upon which the rights and duties are established. For resources plagued by reciprocal externalities, each individual in the resource community has something to gain and something to lose if the rights and duties of property are adhered to. The "I will do X if you will too" structure of the agreement amounts to a quid pro quo. But if some resource users do not impart negative externalities on all others, or if the negative externalities produced by some do not fall alike on all others, a quid pro quo with regard to some users' activities may not be possible. If my use of a resource is quite benign, but yours produces quite extensive externalities, your cessation cannot be traded, as it were, for a similar cessation on my part.

In situations where the externality is nonreciprocal and where it is hard to exclude some users from the deleterious effects of others, either establishing private property rights or making them effective may be quite difficult. Two other factors may also inhibit private property rights from either arising or combating effectively the overuse of a resource. First, establishing property rights and duties is not without cost: information on the status of the resource must be gathered and disseminated; the causes and sources of technological externalities must not only be identified but must also be understood by all to really *be* the cause of the resource's decline; the various decision-making units involved must be brought together to deliberate and agree, and so on. These costs, variously captured under the heading of "costs of negotiation" or "transaction costs,"[53] are perhaps negligible in the case of just two herders who are well informed about the state of their jointly used resource and who are involved in identical and potentially identically destructive activities. However, if we increase the number of decision-making units in the resource community to two *thousand*, and consider much larger resources susceptible to a wide variety of uses, some of which create externalities and some of which do not, then we can imagine that the costs of negotiation might become quite significant indeed.

Second, even if the transaction costs are negligible, so that private property rights can be established quite cheaply, their establishment does not eliminate the incentive for individuals to cheat. Rather, what it does is introduce into each individual's utility calculus an incentive not to, namely, the cost each can expect to incur if they violate their duty.[54] Clearly, then, it is only when the expected costs of violating one's duty exceed the expected benefits of doing so that private property rights will prove an effective solution to commons problems. Barney and Fred can, presumably, easily monitor each other's activities, so that cheating is easy to detect. Each knows this, and each knows also that his cheating is likely to result in a significant reaction of disapproval by the other, which will likely make any short-term gains from the other's cheating quite ethereal.[55] But if it is relatively easy to cheat without getting caught, then the "duty" not to cheat may not actually prevent cheating. If there are hundreds of herders and thousands of cattle, and if the resource is not now a little pasture but an entire region, then cheating may not be so easy to detect. In short, the potentially high costs of policing the agreement and determining when violations have occurred may make the duty to stint seem less compelling and therefore make it easier for people to disregard their duties.

Considerations such as those adduced in the last four paragraphs suggest that the features of private ownership that make its establishment a possible solution to technological externality problems encountered in limited-user open-access situations are more or less operative, depending on various factor endowments of the resource and how it is used. In the situation Hardin asks us to consider, which has been taken by many economists to represent adequately *all* limited-user open access-scenarios, the resource exhibits factor endowments conducive to private ownership: the externalities involved in resource use are reciprocal, the costs of negotiation are rather low, and the expected costs of cheating are quite high. In such "ideal" situations, vesting private property rights in the resource may well be the best way to internalize externalities.

However, in the nonideal situations with which we are concerned, that is, situations where the costs of negotiation are high and the resource exhibits nonreciprocal technological externalities, it may be difficult for members of the resource community to reach any agreement about prudent resource use among themselves. And even if this difficulty can be overcome, the ease of cheating may render any such agreement ineffective for combating technological externalities. In short, in situations that are significantly different from the ones most economists tend to discuss, the costs to the resource community of internalization via privatization may be quite high: to both establish private property rights and to ensure that they are adhered to may take so much time and effort that private ownership becomes simply unworkable. Because economists have tended to conflate and dismiss all forms of common ownership, the only alternative to private ownership that has been seriously considered is state ownership. However, state ownership of resources is discussed disparagingly by most of them.

EXTERNALITIES AND STATE CONTROL

Some economists, recognizing the existence of the sort of nonideal situations with which we are concerned, argue that the control of such resources by an exogenous authority may be the only way to eliminate technological externalities and prevent the resource's depletion and degradation. This authority would operate from outside the resource community, and it would be invested with the power to establish and enforce rules about individuals' use of the resource. Demsetz notes in passing that extensive private property rights may not be effective where the activities that generate negative externalities have multiple sources and impinge unequally upon many people. In such cases, "It may be too costly to internalize effects through the marketplace,"[56] that is, through developing a system of enforceable private property rights. Given other aspects of Demsetz's discussion, the clear implication is that for him, state ownership of resources plagued by nonreciprocal externalities is the only other option available.[57] The father of the so-called property rights school of economics, Ronald H. Coase, echoes Demsetz's sentiments. In one of the most cited economics papers ever written (and in one of the most overlooked portions of that paper), Coase notes that where negotiation and enforcement are likely to be very costly activities, "The government has powers which might enable it to get some things done" better than the marketplace can.[58] That is, the powers of enforcement vested in an authority outside of the resource community may allow it to accomplish what the resource community cannot, namely, make cheating more costly than cooperating. And William Ophuls, who believes that we have entered an unprecedented era of ecological scarcity, one within which private property rights for resources like water in the West must be abandoned altogether, argues that "only a government with the power to regulate individual behavior in the ecological common interest can deal effectively with the tragedy of the commons."[59]

But to most economists, government regulation in any form is rarely if ever an efficient state of affairs. Immediately after touting the advantages of state control, Coase goes on to make the observation that "it will no doubt be commonly the case that the gain which would come from regulating the actions which give rise to [externalities] will be less than the costs involved in government regulation."[60] That is, the empirical evidence indicates that state control of resources tends to become quite expensive "as bureaucracy takes its inevitable toll."[61] Moreover, the nonpecuniary costs that typically accompany government regulation and bureaucracy, those costs that, in the most general terms, negatively affect individuals' freedom, independence, and self-governing values, suggest that state control of resources is an option to be avoided if at all possible. Even advocates of state control, such as Ophuls, recognize the damage to democratic values that typically accompanies the sort of control they advocate for scarce natural resources. Nevertheless, Ophuls thinks that such scarcity "seems to engender overwhelming pressures toward political systems that are frankly authoritarian by current standards, *for there seems to be no other way to check competitive overexploitation of resources. . . .* Leviathan may be mitigated but not evaded."[62]

I have argued that the technological externalities associated with water use in the West are both difficult and costly for individual appropriators to control through private ownership of the resource. Regulating individuals' use of the resource through the government control of western water may work better than private ownership for preventing the degradation and depletion of the resource, but the costs, both pecuniary and otherwise, that typically accompany government regulation suggest that it is an option of last resort. A third option, a common-property arrangement, represents a largely unexplored middle ground between private ownership and state control. Such an arrangement may be a viable way to internalize externalities when the resource is not amenable to being split into individually controlled units. For the most part, economists have not explored adequately enough such arrangements because (1) they have misunderstood what such arrangements look like, (2) they have assumed that individuals act only in ways perceived to be in their own narrow self-interest, and (3) they have tended to focus on the problems associated with reciprocal externalities. In this chapter, we have examined the first and third points; in the next chapter, we will explore the second one more thoroughly.

My thesis can now be stated quite succinctly: In limited-user open-access situations plagued by nonreciprocal externalities, a common-property arrangement may work better than private ownership for combating the degradation and depletion of the resource. As I argue in the final chapter, such an arrangement has the capacity to internalize externalities in ways that a private-property arrangement cannot, and it may be preferable to state control, whose costs, in terms of both dollars spent and liberties lost, make it an unattractive option. In order for a common-property arrangement to be successful, however, there must be a certain amount of trust and willingness among members of the resource community to stint or refrain from free riding voluntarily. If the members of the resource community reach an agreement about prudent resource use, the maintenance of that agreement must rely to some extent on individuals' willingness to abide by that agreement without being coerced into doing so. For the nonideal sorts of resources with which we are concerned, there will still be an incentive for users who impart externalities on others to subsequently break that agreement because such users expect to receive more (or lose less), in the short run at least, by cheating than by cooperating. Common-property arrangements share this feature with limited-user open-access situations: Both states of affairs "contain the incentive for individuals to increase their output beyond the individual share that would produce the joint maximum net product."[63] We have been assuming that one feature of the nonideal sorts of resources we are concerned with is that the costs of compulsory enforcement are quite high, and that is what promises to make private property rights rather ineffective in such situations. This suggests that to be successful, common-property arrangements must rely to a large extent on some self-reinforcing, noncompulsory enforcement mechanism(s). We need to first understand the particular logical features of such a mechanism, and we need to then investigate the technological and sociological conditions within which the individual members of a resource community can be expected to act accordingly.

NOTES

1. Terry L. Anderson and P. J. Hill, "The Evolution of Property Rights: A Study of the American West," *Journal of Law and Economics* 18 (1975), 165; see also Glenn G. Stevenson, *Common Property Economics: A General Theory and Land Use Applications* (Cambridge: Cambridge University Press, 1991), 58.

2. See Daniel W. Bromley, *Environment and Economy: Property Rights and Public Policy* (Oxford: Basil Blackwell, 1991), 4; and Daniel W. Bromley, "The Commons, Property, and Common-Property Regimes," in *Making the Commons Work*, ed. Daniel W. Bromley et al. (San Francisco: Institute for Contemporary Studies, 1992), 5–7.

3. Ronald H. Coase was referring to A. C. Pigou's *The Economics of Welfare* (1932), which, from the time of its publication early in this century, had been taken as orthodoxy among welfare economists. Not really understanding it, Coase argued, most economists did not understand that it was wrong. See Coase, "The Problem of Social Cost," *Law and Economics* 3 (October 1960): 39–44; see also H. Scott Bierman and Luis Fernandez, *Game Theory with Economic Applications* (Reading, MA: Addison-Wesley, 1993), 217–218.

4. See Amartya K. Sen, "Isolation, Assurance and the Social Rate of Discount," *Quarterly Journal of Economics* 81 (1967): 112–113; Stevenson, *Common Property Economics*, 20–27; and C. Ford Runge, "Common Property and Collective Action in Economic Development," in *Making the Com-*

mons Work, ed. Daniel W. Bromley et al. (San Francisco: Institute for Contemporary Studies, 1992), 21–27.

5. Stevenson, *Common Property Economics*, 1.

6. Garrett Hardin, "The Tragedy of the Commons," *Science* 162 (1968), reprinted in *Managing the Commons*, ed. Garrett Hardin and John Baden (New York: Freeman, 1977), 20 (page citations are to the reprint edition).

7. Ibid.

8. Ibid.

9. S. V. Ciriacy-Wantrup and Richard C. Bishop, "'Common Property' as a Concept in Natural Resources Policy," *Natural Resources Journal* 15, no. 4 (1975): 715.

10. See Ronald J. Oakerson, "Analyzing the Commons: A Framework," in *Making the Commons Work*, ed. Daniel W. Bromley et al. (San Francisco: Institute for Contemporary Studies, 1992), 49–51; and Stevenson, *Common Property Economics*, 52–53.

11. See Hardin, "Tragedy of the Commons," 22, 27.

12. Douglas North and Robert P. Thomas, "The First Economic Revolution," *Economic History Review* 30 (1977): 234; see also Runge, "Common Property and Collective Action," 20; Stevenson, *Common Property Economics*, 39n; and Bromley, *Environment and Economy*, 137.

13. Demsetz, "Toward a Theory of Property Rights," 354, 356.

14. Stevenson, *Common Property Economics*, 1.

15. Demsetz, "Toward a Theory of Property Rights," 355.

16. For similar comments, see Stevenson, *Common Property Economics*, 59.

17. See Stevenson, *Common Property Economics*, 52–59.

18. Bromley, "Commons, Property, and Common-Property Regimes," 4.

19. The Swiss grazing commons are discussed at length by Stevenson, *Common Property Economics*, chapters 4 and 5; the marine coastal fisheries of Turkey are examined by Fikret Berkes, "Success and Failure in Marine Coastal Fisheries of Turkey," in *Making the Commons Work*, ed. Daniel W. Bromley et al. (San Francisco: Institute for Contemporary Studies, 1992), 161–182; and irrigation systems are discussed by Bromley, "Commons, Property, and Common-Property Regimes," 11–12, and Bromley, *Environment and Economy*, 149–150; see also Ciriacy-Wantrup and Bishop, "Common Property," 717–721.

20. Stevenson, *Common Property Economics*, 46; see also Ciriacy-Wantrup and Bishop, "Common Property," 714; and Bromley, *Environment and Economy*, 25–30.

21. Stevenson, *Common Property Economics*, 2, 8, 20–27.

22. That they each originally own the same number of cattle is not significant. As we will see shortly, the same conclusion would be reached even if one of them owned many more cattle than did the other.

23. The assumption of a constant diminution in the value of the cattle above the pasture's carrying capacity is quite conservative and overly opti-

mistic. It would be more realistic to assume a sharp increase in the marginal costs as more and more animals are added above the pasture's carrying capacity. However, this "best case" scenario serves to illustrate the main point; making it more realistic would only strengthen the conclusion. For a graphic model that makes more realistic assumptions about marginal costs, see Stevenson, *Common Property Economics*, 14–20.

24. See Ciriacy-Wantrup and Bishop, "Common Property," 719.

25. It does not matter if we think of Fred and Barney as individual persons or as other entities, such as individual firms or corporations, or if we think of one of them as an individual and the other one as a firm or a corporation. The key is that each entity is a *decision-making unit* that reasons and acts only in its own perceived *self-interest*.

26. We can see now that the fact that Barney and Fred originally own the same number of animals is not important. As long as Barney originally owned less than ninety-nine of the cattle, he would have an incentive to add another animal, because by doing so he would gain more than he lost.

27. See Sen, "Isolation, Assurance, and the Social Rate of Discount," 112–113; and Stevenson, *Common Property Economics,* 22–27.

28. Hardin, "Tragedy of the Commons," 20.

29. Sen, "Isolation, Assurance, and the Social Rate of Discount, 112–113.

30. Ibid.

31. Bromley, *Environment and Economy*, 59.

32. Though, of course, Fred himself is a net loser here ($4,950 versus $4,998), which is why, under the Prisoner's Dilemma scenario, neither he nor anyone else will decide to stint of his or her own accord.

33. See Bromley, *Environment and Economy*, 71–73.

34. Ibid., 69.

35. See Demsetz, "Toward a Theory of Property Rights," 347.

36. See Bromley, *Environment and Economy*, 49, 69.

37. As Hardin says, "The pollution problem is a consequence of population. It did not much matter how a lonely American frontiersman disposed of his waste. 'Flowing water purifies itself every ten miles,' my grandfather used to say, and the myth was near enough to the truth when he was a boy, for there were not too many people." See Hardin, "Tragedy of the Commons," 22.

38. See Hardin, "The Tragedy of the Commons," 21–22; Stevenson, *Common Property Economics*, 44; and Bromley, "Commons, Property, and Common-Property Regimes," 14–15.

39. See Demsetz, "Toward a Theory of Property Rights," 348.

40. Stevenson, *Common Property Economics*, 43.

41. "Alike" does *not* mean "equally." A herder with sixty animals will not be affected as much as a herder with only five animals; a farmer twenty miles away from a smoke-spewing factory will not suffer as much as the farmer two miles closer to the factory.

42. See Stevenson, *Common Property Economics*, 43.

43. For a discussion of the externality problems associated with water pollution, see S. V. Ciriacy-Wantrup, "Water Quality, A Problem for the Economist," *Journal of Farm Economics* 153 (1961): 1133–1144. For a characterization of water pollution as a nonreciprocal (or as he calls it, an asymmetric) negative externality, see Stevenson, *Common Property Economics*, 9.

44. Even those who are in favor of common-property arrangements for certain resources tend to confine their analyses to cases where there are only reciprocal externalities. See Stevenson, *Common Property Economics*, 9, 44.

45. Bromley, "Commons, Property, and Common-Property Regimes," 21; see also Sen, "Isolation, Assurance, and the Social Rate of Discount," 113.

46. As was discussed earlier in this chapter, solving the problem need not mean eliminating it; rather, it only means that economics has nothing further to say about the matter.

47. Demsetz, "Toward a Theory of Property," 350.

48. Bromley, "Commons, Property, and Common-Property Regimes," 4. Economists actually go one logical step further, maintaining that the *concept* of property can in effect be understood wholly in terms of property rights and duties. This is because the relevant benefits and costs involved are wholly captured by the conjunction of rights and duties; that is, all the value of property is reflected in the various property *rights*. As Demsetz puts it, "A bundle of rights often attaches to a physical commodity or service, but it is the value of the rights that determines the value of what is exchanged." See Demsetz, "Toward a Theory of Property," 347.

49. See Hardin, "Tragedy of the Commons," 22, 27.

50. See chapters three and four.

51. Given the scenario I sketched earlier in this chapter, we can see that Fred would be willing to pay up to $3.99 to build a fence. But we should notice that under some systems of property rights, it might be Barney who decides to build a fence instead. If Barney were made liable for the full social costs of his "trespass"—allowing his cattle to roam on Fred's land—*he* would be willing to pay the $3.99 in order to avoid being sued. For a discussion of liability rules and property rules as entitlement guarantees, see Coase, "Problem of Social Cost"; and Bromley, *Environment and Economy*, 41–54.

52. If the degradation to his half of the pasture causes the value of each of his fifty original animals to fall by $2, then he receives $98 for adding the fifty-first animal, but he loses $100.

53. See Stevenson, *Common Property Economics*, 70; and Coase, "Problem of Social Cost," 15.

54. See Stevenson, *Common Property Economics*, 71–73.

55. See chapter 3 for both a discussion of possible responses to and individuals' violations of his or her moral or legal duties.

56. Demsetz, "Toward a Theory of Property," 357.

57. See Stevenson, *Common Property Economics*, 59.

58. Coase, "Problem of Social Cost," 17.

59. Ophuls, "Ecology and the Politics of Scarcity Revisited," 204.

60. Ibid., 18.

61. Robert B. Hawkins, Forward to *Making the Commons Work*, ed. Daniel W. Bromley et al. (San Francisco: Institute for Contemporary Studies, 1992), xi.

62. Ophuls, "Ecology and the Politics of Scarcity Revisited," 216.

63. Ibid., 57.

6

Toward a Common-Property Arrangement for Water in the West

No matter how diverse and complex the patterns of livelihood may be that arise within the river system, no matter how many the perspectives from which people view the basin, no matter how diversely they value it, it is, finally, one and the same river for everyone, and if we all want to stay here, in some kind of relation to the river, then we have to learn, somehow, to live together.
Daniel Kemmis, *Community and the Politics of Place*

INTRODUCTION

In a Prisoner's Dilemma, it is assumed that each player decides what to do regardless of what others might decide, and that each player's decision is motivated only by narrow self-interest. Given these stipulations, free riding emerges as the strictly dominant strategy for each player. If an analogue of the Prisoner's Dilemma is the appropriate model for analyzing problems associated with resources plagued by nonreciprocal externalities, then a strong external authority with the power to discourage free riding effectively may be the only way to combat the degradation and depletion of such resources. The palpable threat of discovery and punishment by that authority makes the expected costs of free riding higher than the expected benefits, and strict compliance to any agreed-upon rights and duties becomes the rational course of action for each user of the resource. Hence, as William Ophuls concludes, "The rationale for government with major coercive powers is overwhelming."[1]

However, if free riding is *not* the strictly dominant strategy for individuals confronted with public goods scenarios, then there may be institutional arrangements other than a strong external authority for combating the depletion and degradation of resources like water in the West. And there are good reasons for believing that the Prisoner's Dilemma model is, in fact, a misleading representation of the choice function facing individuals in such situations. Experiments in the social sciences over the last quarter century have shown repeatedly that the free-rider hypothesis is contradicted by people's actual behavior. In such experiments, "people voluntarily contribute substantial portions of their resources . . . to the provision of a public good. This despite the fact that the conditions of the experiments are expressly designed to maximize the probability of individualized, self-interested behavior."[2] Even though these experiments are designed as Prisoner's Dilemmas, it appears that positing strictly dominant strategies to free ride do not explain the results. While a rigorous analytical explanation of such behavior does not currently exist, the fact that free riding often is not the strictly dominant strategy in such situations indicates that the Prisoner's Dilemma is an inadequate picture of individuals' choice functions in public goods scenarios.

One explanation for the apparently irrational behavior of the players in such situations is that individuals have a preference for cooperation that transcends narrow self-interest, a preference that can sometimes serve to drive a wedge between personal choice and personal welfare.[3] Such a preference can be captured in the Assurance Game, which therefore represents a more accurate picture of an individual's choice function in public goods situations than is offered by the Prisoner's Dilemma. In an Assurance Game, an individual's choice of behavior *is* affected by others' behavior—or more accurately by *expectations* of others' behavior—and that choice *can* be motivated by concerns going *beyond* narrow self-interest. The players in an Assurance Game have a willingness to practice self-restraint voluntarily if each has enough assurance that enough others will practice self-restraint as well. This willingness may be motivated by self-interest, but it may also be motivated by a preference for cooperation, or *coordinated activity*, as such, a preference that goes beyond narrow self-interest. Whereas in a Prisoner's Dilemma no one will voluntarily contribute to the provision of a public good even if everyone else does, in the Assurance Game this is no longer the case because each player's choice of behavior is affected by expectations of others' choices.[4] In the next section, I discuss the Assurance Game and show how the preference for coordinated activity within it can be rendered in a way that is suitable to the case of water in the West.

In the Assurance Game, free riding is still an option, but it no longer strictly dominates cooperating. An individual resource user's decision to cooperate is conditional on his or her expectations of others' cooperation. If, however, only *total* assurance of *all others'* cooperation will be enough to motivate an individual's cooperation, then we will not have gained much by moving from the Prisoner's Dilemma to the Assurance Game. With the case of water in the West, providing every resource user with that level of assurance is either impossible or impossibly expensive, and we might as well just carry on as if free riding were in fact the strictly dominate strategy. But if enough resource users prefer to cooperate even in cases where there is less than total assurance of total compliance, then there may be more realistic and attainable situations where conditional cooperation will manifest itself and the resource will be improved. Results of social experiments show not only that free riding is not strictly dominant, but also that some players will choose to practice self-restraint even when they expect some other players to cheat. As Elinor Ostrom and James Walker discovered in their experiments, "Several groups overtly faced the problem of small levels of nonconformance, and decided to keep to their agreement as long as the level of deviation did not get too large."[5] This preference corresponds to a *commitment* to cooperate, a commitment that remains operative even when some individuals in a group can be expected to free ride anyway. Where such commitments can be activated and maintained, public goods can be provided without guaranteeing to each resource user the total compliance of all others. And if less than total compliance is required for enough individuals to stick to their agreement, then something less than the powers of a centralized state authority may be sufficient for solving some public goods problems.

Later on, I discuss how in an effective community the requisite initiative for enough individuals to cooperate voluntarily may be activated and maintained without reliance on an external enforcement mechanism. When people have a common goal, when they have stable and direct relations with one another so that they can discuss that goal, and when they are capable of practicing generalized reciprocity in order to achieve that goal, then they constitute an effective community. As such, the group may be able to generate enough confi-

dence in one another such that the commitment to cooperate flour-
ishes, and there will then be a much reduced need to continually
enforce their agreements: as their confidence in one another's expected behavior increases, their need for coercive enforcement can be
expected to decrease. And if there is enough confidence among members of a community, achieving the required level of monitoring and
enforcement may be well within the means of the community itself.

Within the Assurance Game, expectations about others' cooperation affect one's own cooperation, and one's own cooperation, in turn,
affects others' expectations. This model of conditional, *self-reinforcing* cooperation is the appropriate one for discussing solutions to
some public goods problems, including those encountered by water
users in the American West. The requisite level of conditional cooperation can be achieved there within a suitably constructed resource
community if it is possible to generate and maintain a high degree of
confidence among its members. Later on, I discuss how these conditions either already exist or can be created in the Colorado River basin, and how, therefore, a communal approach to managing water
resources in the region may be successful. I argue that the success of
a common-property arrangement for water in the West will rely
heavily on a multitude of small-scale, local, and personalized social
institutions, which, in order to function effectively, will themselves
require the widespread and active participation of the basin's inhabitants. Rather than continuing to act as so many separate, self-interested decision-making units, the basin's inhabitants will have to
identify themselves with and come to operate as more intimately
connected parts of a larger, interconnected whole.

Such a picture evokes a notion of political obligation often associated with the civic republican tradition in political theory. Civic republicans take a face-to-face, hands-on approach to problem solving;
they advocate small-scale, participatory units of government, where
individuals are engaged with one another directly, intensively, and
repeatedly enough to come to know and desire the common good.
And for civic republicans, "If compulsion is necessary, local and de-
centralized authority is more acceptable than direction from a remote centralized source of power."[6] In the final section, I discuss how
the overall character of an effective resource community maps onto
this civic republican conception of political obligation, such that a
common-property arrangement for water in the West would, in effect, constitute a water republic. Insofar as a common-property arrangement constitutes one vision of a political theory with a rich
tradition in political thought, Ophuls's contention that, in the face of

the sort of ecological scarcity westerners are confronting, we need "a new paradigm of politics," and that "democracy as we know it cannot conceivably survive,"[7] is simply overblown.

THE ASSURANCE GAME

Unlike their counterparts confronted with a Prisoner's Dilemma, the players in an Assurance Game have a preference for coordinating their activities with one another.[8] Rendering this preference so that it is adequate for the case of water in the West is the burden of this section, but if individuals are endowed with even a minimal desire to cooperate with one another, we can see how potential free riders might instead choose a different strategy. The assurance that others will honor their agreement to contribute to a common goal *can*, by itself, significantly influence many individuals to act accordingly. Similarly, the assurance that others will renege on their agreement may influence individuals to free ride. In either case, since among an individual's preferences is the preference for coordinating his or her own activities with the activities of others, expectations about other players' activities come to play an important role in an individual player's choice function. As we are able to strengthen individuals' expectations of others' compliance with an agreement about prudent resource use, the likelihood of those individuals' voluntary compliance increases. And if voluntary compliance can be sufficiently motivated and sustained within a resource community, then there is a reduced need for continually enforcing any agreed-upon use restrictions.

The main reason for adopting the Assurance Game is that it models individuals' choice functions in public goods situations better than does the Prisoner's Dilemma. However, some have argued that there is no reason to turn to a different choice function in order to explain cooperative behavior; rather, they argue that the fact that individuals often adapt their behavior to expectations about others' behavior can be captured in *repeated plays* of the Prisoner's Dilemma. For example, Glenn G. Stevenson writes, "The problem of assurance can be modeled within the original context of the prisoner's dilemma by allowing adjustment of individual strategies once the other player's move is known."[9] In other words, the *iterated* Prisoner's Dilemma, rather than the one-shot variety, is the proper framework for considering public goods situations. In an iterated Prisoner's Dilemma, each player discovers that his or her defection in an earlier round of the game instigates others' defection in subsequent rounds, and, over time, each will eventually come to practice cooperation. That is, given the assurance of restraint on the part of others, together with the assurance that defection on one's part will simply cause others to defect as well, each will come to practice self-restraint for self-interested reasons alone. The incentive to free ride is still present in the iterated Prisoner's Dilemma; it is just that the incentive not to free ride is greater.

While the iterated Prisoner's Dilemma is a more reasonable model of public goods situations than is the one-shot variety, even an iterated version of it fails to capture adequately the variety of incentives that may be important to explanations of public goods contributions.[10] Early developers of the iterated Prisoner's Dilemma recognized this; Martin Shubik, for one, remarked, "For most problems of interest [the iterated Prisoner's Dilemma] is not rich enough to capture a useful abstraction of human affairs."[11] Even Stevenson, at the end of his discussion of the iterated Prisoner's Dilemma, finds it necessary to add into the picture "the real-world desires of individuals to conform to group norms."[12] Such desires are nowhere reflected in the Prisoner's Dilemma model. So, although the iterated Prisoner's Dilemma may better represent the real world than does the one-shot variety, a model that explicitly includes the preference for coordinated activity may represent it better still. With this in mind, we can turn to an examination of the extent of this preference.

We can begin discussing the preference structure of players in an Assurance Game by first considering whether it is a preference only for *universal cooperation*. As such, for any individual resource user R, given the choice between (1) everyone contributing to the common good and (2) everyone *except R* contributing, R prefers the former over the latter. At least in the special case where everyone else does contribute to a common good, R now prefers to contribute to it as well. As some have characterized the Assurance Game, it is only in this special case where an individual will actually contribute a substantial portion of his or her resources to the provision of a public good. Amartya K. Sen, who was the first to discuss the Assurance Game explicitly, writes, "excepting this special case, the individual continues to prefer [free riding] to [contributing] no matter what the others do."[13] In a similar vein, Jon Elster maintains that "the slightest uncertainty or suspicion will make an actor choose [to free ride] rather than [to contribute]."[14]

If this is the extent of the preference for cooperation modeled in the Assurance Game, then such a model is only marginally better than the Prisoner's Dilemma: The Assurance Game does allow for the possibility that individuals would choose to contribute voluntarily to the provision of a common good, but the conditions under which they would be so motivated are too restrictive. Such conditions are not likely to be brought about for the sort of public goods scenarios with which I am concerned. In the case of the Colorado River basin, where there are millions of water users spread out over hundreds of thousands of square miles, there will most certainly be some measure of uncertainty about others' behavior: complete assurance cannot be guaranteed, everyone will attempt to free ride, and the resource will continue to be degraded and depleted.

However, neither Sen nor Elster give any reasons why they think the preference for cooperation can be activated only when an individual is *completely assured of all others' compliance*. As I mentioned earlier, experimental results support the contention that even when faced with some amount of uncertainty, and some expectation that others will free ride anyway, individuals often still choose to contribute voluntarily to the provision of a public good. So, if the Assurance Game is to be a useful abstraction of an individual's behavior with regard to his or her use of public goods, then the conditions for cooperation within the game must be expanded to encompass more than just the special case of universal cooperation.[15]

Even if individuals have a preference for only universal cooperation, this introduces a moral component into their choice function, a moral component that players in either the one-shot or iterated versions of the Prisoner's Dilemma lack. Individuals playing the Assurance Game sometimes prefer to cooperate voluntarily, that is, practice self-restraint, not because they think the costs of free riding will outweigh its benefits, even in the long run, but, rather, because they think cooperating is, in some other sense, the *right* thing to do. More specifically, they consider their self-restraint to be "right" when they expect that enough others will practice self-restraint too.[16] In the special case Sen and Elster discuss, *all* other players must be expected to practice self-restraint. But more generally, it is an individual's expectations of *some* others' cooperative behavior that establishes for that individual the rightness of cooperating as well.

The preference for cooperation, whether universal or nonuniversal, can be usefully considered as the (moral) preference for *conditional cooperation*. The rationale for universal cooperation can be represented by the statement: I am willing to do X if everyone else will also do X. In this form, the preference for coordinated activity denotes a preference not only for universal cooperation, but also for everyone's *equal* cooperation, or *everyone doing* (or *expected* to be doing) *the same thing*. C. Ford Runge, in describing what motivates individuals in the Assurance Game to cooperate, labels it "fair-mindedness," which he characterizes "simply as the preference for *equal contribution*, whether this contribution is large, small, or zero. This preference can be either in favor of or against contribution—depending on what is expected of others."[17] Runge cites with approval experimental results showing that small levels of free riding need not undermine voluntary cooperation in all situations, implying that the expectations of roughly equal contributions by others in his account are meant to be nonuniversal. The rationale for conditional cooperation in Runge's case would, then, take the form: I will do X if I am *relatively certain that enough others* will also do X, where "enough others" need not mean *all* others.

Even so, this level of fair-mindedness is still insufficient for the case of water in the West. There, different resource users differently use the resource such that farmer *A*'s cooperative behavior, in terms of improving the quantity or quality of the resource, might *not* be the same as farmer *B*'s, and probably neither one's behavior will resemble the sort of behavior that an urban dweller *U* can be expected to exhibit. Suppose that *A* farms two hundred acres of a water-intensive crop on very salty soil, whereas *B* grows a much less water-intensive crop on fewer and more fertile acres, but does so with an ancient and inefficient irrigation system. We should expect that, insofar as *A* and *B* are willing to contribute to the improvement of the resource, each must change his or her activities in rather different ways. Whereas *A* must address his soil/crop problem, *B* must address her irrigation system. And *U*'s expected behavior, in both scope and character, will be different still—perhaps *U* will have to give up his or her plush lawn or swimming pool. More generally, because the externalities exhibited by water use in the West are of a nonreciprocal nature, expectations of roughly equal contributions among even a critical mass of users cannot be generated with certainty. If the preference for coordinated activity in the Assurance Game is a preference only for roughly equal, though nonuniversal, contribution, then the Assurance Game will not provide us with an adequate basis for discussing an internal solution to the West's water woes.

The expectations necessary for the users of western water to generate enough cooperation and voluntary self-restraint among themselves must, then, include expectations of the *nonuniversal* and substantially *unequal* contributions of others. In particular, individual users must be willing to do the right thing even if they expect to practice more or even a different sort of self-restraint than they expect a critical mass of others to practice. Under the right conditions, which I will discuss, it might be possible to generate and sustain sufficiently this level of commitment within a resource community. But even under the appropriate conditions, if this sort of commitment looks too much like *altruism*, then we will be forced to confront several theoretical, empirical, and intuitive difficulties.

It is both less problematic and, I think, more accurate to consider this willingness to do the right thing as a form of *reciprocity*, roughly corresponding to what Michael Taylor calls *generalized reciprocity*.[18] As distinguished from merely equal or balanced reciprocity, the rationale for generalized reciprocity takes the form: I will do X if I am relatively certain that a critical mass of other people will do Y, where X and Y can represent quite different levels or even kinds of self-restraining behavior. Whereas the preference to behave altruistically often involves a desire to contribute *regardless* of others' expected behavior,[19] the preference for generalized reciprocity is always conditional on such expectations. Strictly speaking then, the sort of conditional cooperation required for the case of water in the West should not be thought of as a form of altruism. It is better understood as a (moral) preference for generalized reciprocity.[20]

By including among individuals' preferences a preference for generalized reciprocity, we are in effect saying that individuals are endowed with a certain amount of *reasonableness*. "Reasonable persons," John Rawls writes, "are not moved by the general good as such but desire for its own sake a social world in which they . . . can cooperate with others on terms all can accept."[21] In Rawls's account, reasonable persons exhibit a moral sensibility lying somewhere between the altruistic desire to promote the general good and the selfish desire to promote only their own well being. He describes this moral sensibility as the desire for reciprocity: "The reasonable is an element of the idea of society as a system of fair cooperation and that its fair terms be reasonable for all to accept is part of its idea of reciprocity."[22] Fair terms of cooperation need not mean only equal terms; what is considered a fair contribution to a public good may differ from one individual to another, depending on each individual's current patterns of resource use. That is, reasonable persons have the capacity to be moved to contribute to the provision of a public good when generalized, rather than merely equal, reciprocal behavior can be expected of others.

Reasonable persons are willing to practice generalized reciprocity because doing so is (sometimes) an integral part of the maintenance of the social order. Where the provision of a public good is a desirable aspect of that social order, people have a preference or motivation to try to cooperate with one another in order to provide that good. When the good can be provided by an equal contribution by all, then a preference for merely balanced reciprocity may be sufficient for providing that good. But in situations where unequal contributions are required to provide the good in question, a more vague and diffuse sort of reciprocity is required. A person who is willing to contribute to the provision of a public good where others' contributions are neither guaranteed nor expected to be the same as their own need not be cast as either a saint or a sucker.[23] Rather, such individuals may simply have a more expansive idea of reciprocity, one in which "fair" cooperation signifies something different than equal cooperation by everyone. While it may not be wholly rational, that is, in my narrow self-interest, for me to do my share when I expect that others' share will amount to something less than my own, it may nonetheless not be unreasonable for me to do so. That sentiment, I think, can be part of an Assurance Game, and it can be the factor that may prove equal to the task of motivating individuals to work voluntarily toward the improvement of a public good like water in the West. The main problem in such situations is not, then, figuring out how to make the expected costs of free riding higher than the expected costs of cooperating; it is instead figuring out how to generate the requisite level of expectations so that individuals' preference for coordinated activity, or their (moral) capacity for reasonable behavior, can be rendered operative.

Before going on to discuss how such expectations might in fact be activated and maintained among a group of resource users, I want to touch briefly on one other aspect of the Assurance Game as I have characterized it. One might argue that some people prefer to contribute voluntarily to the improvement of a public good only because they perceive that their own well being *will* thereby be improved, though improved in ways falling outside of traditional economic analysis. Although in strictly economic or pecuniary terms the resource user expects to be worse off by cooperating, such losses are more than offset by expectations of other, nonpecuniary gains. Perhaps the resource user expects to be able to sleep better at night, or otherwise expects to feel better off psychologically or emotionally, simply because he or she has improved others' situation. In other words, it is not the preference for coordinated activity as such that motivates some individuals to contribute when some others contribute either nothing or nothing of the same magnitude; rather, it is simply a case of *sympathy*. And, some have argued, behavior based on sympathy is in an important sense self-interested behavior, "For one is oneself pleased at others' pleasure and pained at others' pain, and the pursuit of one's own utility may thus be helped by sympathetic action."[24] The implication here is that we do not need a model like the Assurance Game to explain significant levels of cooperation in the face of either uncertainty or low levels of free riding; rather, we only need to reformulate the Prisoner's Dilemma, either in its one-shot or iterated form, so that nonpecuniary benefits are included in an individual player's choice function.

Because we lack a rigorous analytical explanation as to why free riding is not the strictly dominant strategy in social science experiments designed to model public goods scenarios, it must be left as an open question whether it is sympathy or the preference for coordinated activity—or something else altogether—that can best explain the results. Based on nothing better than my own intuitions and experiences, however, I think that sympathy is by itself too precarious a concept on which to base political arguments and to construct effective social institutions. Moreover, the move to explain self-restraining behavior in terms of self-interest alone just seems patently false—or vacuous, if "self-interest" can be expanded to cover *any* motive that might be identified.[25] Be that as it may, I also think that for sympathy to operate effectively, the same conditions must be present as are required for conditional cooperation to work. Only if people have both common interests and direct and multifaceted relations with one another can either sympathy or conditional cooperation work effectively to combat the depletion and degradation of jointly used resources plagued by nonreciprocal externalities. So, while sympathy may ultimately turn out to be the correct explanation for self-restraining behavior, sufficiently motivating such sympathy would still seem to require the sort of background conditions that will be discussed.

EFFECTIVE COMMUNITIES

It seems reasonable to maintain that among an individual's preferences is the preference for coordinated activity, or conditional cooperation, as such. In cases of public goods provision generally, this preference translates into an individual's willingness to contribute to the improvement of a resource when he or she has enough assurance that enough others are willing to contribute to it as well. In the specific case of water use in the Colorado River basin, where such contributions are expected to be neither equal nor universal, the activation of this preference to a degree sufficient for the improvement of the resource must, to a large extent, rely on individuals' willingness to practice conditional cooperation in the form of generalized reciprocity. This willingness will manifest itself only when the individual users come to see themselves as part of an *effective community*. In this section, I describe such communities and outline the general background conditions that make them possible.

"Community," writes Alan Gewirth, "signifies the institutionalized social bond that unites persons by virtue of their society's fulfillment of important needs and their mutual contributions thereto."[26] When a group of individuals see themselves as members of a community, a commitment to generalized reciprocity can perhaps be activated and maintained, and an internal solution to public goods provision is therefore possible. This initial characterization of "community" is, however, inadequate; not all resource communities are equally effective, that is, equally capable of generating the requisite level of a commitment to conditional cooperation. A common-property arrangement for water in the Colorado River basin represents an internal solution based on the activation and maintenance of such a commitment. Therefore, the viability of such an arrangement depends on creating an effective resource community. We need some way to distinguish effective communities from ineffective ones.

Even by restricting the discussion to situations involving only human agents, as contrasted with those involving other living organisms, because we typically apply the term "community" to such a wide variety of things and states of affairs, there is not, and perhaps cannot be, an exhaustive specification of the conditions for the correct use of "community." As Taylor points out, "Neighbourhoods, villages, towns, cities, nations and ethnic groups are all spoken of as communities; there are monastic, utopian, and other 'intentional' communities; there are 'the academic community,' 'the business community' and a host of other specialized communities."[27] To this already diverse collection we could also add the sorts of "virtual communities" made possible by advances in computing and telecommunications. The point is that "community" appears to be an open-textured concept; attempts to specify both necessary and sufficient conditions for it always come up short. We may be able to identify communities when we see them, but we may not be able to say up front exactly what it is that we are looking for: what we mean by the term changes from one context to another.

Nevertheless, we can and often do speak of *this* state of affairs as being *more* of a community than *that* one is. Certainly, it makes at least some sense to say that a small, closely knit group of individuals living together in a commune is *more like* what we typically think of as a community than is a large, loosely knit, and far-flung collection of businessmen and -women who interact only narrowly and infrequently, perhaps only on conference calls and at sales seminars. The former state of affairs connotes a *stronger* sense of community than does the latter; we expect that the members of the former sort of community will be better able to reach and keep agreements about their behavior than will the members of the latter sort. The main difference between the two states of affairs concerns the overall character of the members' relationship to one another. In a commune, the members share an almost complete consensus on a wide range of beliefs and values, and their relationship to one another is both direct and multifaceted. In the business community, the members share a more limited set of beliefs and values, and their relationship to one another is relatively indirect and largely one-dimensional. More generally, we can say that when a group of individuals is characterized by many common beliefs and values and when their relationship to one another is direct and many-sided, that group constitutes more of a community, or a stronger community, than does a group that, in relative terms, lacks such features. While some states of affairs we would probably not want to call communities might also exhibit such features, none of the things we commonly identify as a "community" lack them altogether.[28] All communities exhibit these characteristics, some of them to a greater degree than others. It is those communities that exhibit a high degree of these characteristics that have the potential for being effective communities.

The impetus for distinguishing communities along these lines is that it is only when a group of individuals exhibits a strong sense of community that the sorts of social mechanisms that represent an alternative to continual and coercive enforcement can work effectively. Rather than relying mainly on the coercive force of the state to change the payoffs and thus the desirability of free-riding behavior, an effective communal solution to public goods provision relies to a large degree on the persuasive and diffuse influence of other community members' expected behavior to activate individuals' preference for and commitment to coordinated activity or conditional cooperation. In an effective community, it is the overall influence of the expectation of other members' actions that motivates individuals to cooperate as well, and not the threat of immediate and palpable reaction by a single, powerful entity. Previously, I characterized such cooperative behavior as a manifestation of the moral sensibility or preference for doing the right thing. Where others' doing the right thing can effectively influence enough individuals to cooperate, we have a community capable of generating the requisite level of self-restraint to combat the overuse of a public good. In order for others' doing the right thing to influence an individual's choice of behavior, that individual not only must be cognizant of others' behavior, he or she also must see the "rightness" of such behavior. When the relationship among resource users is direct and multifaceted, it is not difficult to be cognizant of others' behavior, and when there is a consensus among the users about their beliefs and values vis-à-vis the resource, it is relatively easy to determine what counts as doing the right thing. So, the greater degree to which a group of resource users exhibits the characteristics of a strong community, the more effective they may be in providing a public good without an external enforcement mechanism. Strong communities have the potential for being effective communities, ones within which the activation of individuals' moral sensibilities can result in generalized reciprocal behavior.

Within an effective community, the actions of each of its members are relatively public, that is, open for all to see for themselves, and those actions are evaluated in both moral and nonmoral terms. It is not simply that an individual's noncooperative behavior may have harmful pecuniary effects on others. It is also the case that such behavior is considered to be *morally* wrong. Obviously, we cannot expect that an individual's recognition that his or her own behavior is morally wrong will, by itself, motivate a change in that behavior. But we can and should expect that when others see that an individual is continuing to act wrongly, their attitude toward that individual will change: that individual's *reputation* may be diminished; the *esteem* with which he or she is held may erode; and/or *gossip* about and *derision* of that individual may become quite pervasive. In short, the pressure of public opinion may result in various forms of social *ostracism*, such that the noncooperator loses his or her standing in the community and is no longer able to function as an effective member of it. By acting wrongly, an individual displays contempt for the beliefs and values of the community, and the shame and ridicule engendered by others' expression of that contempt are often effective means for modifying an individual's behavior.[29] In communities where relations among individuals are marked by a commonality of beliefs about right and wrong actions, and where relations among the members are direct and multifaceted, there may be quite effective social mechanisms for motivating noncooperators to change their cheating ways.

There will, of course, be those individuals who are rather oblivious to such forms of persuasion, and who will continue to act wrongly unless actually forced to act otherwise by credible threats of coercion. The rest of the community then has two choices: either it can choose to use coercive measures to enforce compliance, or it can refrain from doing so. We should reiterate here that we are centrally concerned with a specific sort of community, one whose purpose is the improvement of a jointly used resource plagued by nonreciprocal externalities. In many cases, complete compliance is not required for improving the resource: as long as only a few people choose to free ride, enough of the good may be provided so that the community as a whole is better off. If the actions of a few free riders will not undermine the community's goal, then the other members of the community might just allow those individuals to go on acting wrongly—though the bulk of the community will probably ostracize those free riders in the ways discussed in the last paragraph. However, the danger in doing so is that allowing free-riding behavior to go uncorrected may well precipitate others to free ride too, and that the community's purpose *will* in fact be undermined. Where moral persuasion in its various guises is not enough to cause free riders to change their ways, such mechanisms will have to be augmented by some form(s) of coercive enforcement. In addition, then, to strong values and beliefs and a high degree of direct interaction among its members, an effective resource community will most likely have to have effective means for changing the pecuniary payoffs of those who might choose to free ride.

A resource community is not rendered ineffective simply by the fact that some coercive measures might need to be taken against some of its members. Rather, the community becomes ineffective when the required enforcement mechanisms are beyond the community's means. These enforcement mechanisms fall into two general categories: detection and correction. With regard to the first, we have been explicitly assuming that an individual's activities vis-à-vis the resource are open to public scrutiny; this is an aspect of the high degree of directness and many-sidedness of the members' relationships with one another. In such a situation, the detection mechanism is, in effect, distributed throughout the community, which, then, need not have to create and maintain a centralized institution for detecting free riding. Or, in the relative terms in which most of the discussion in this section has so far been couched, we could say that the more open individuals' activities are to scrutiny by others, the less need there will be for the community's investment in a detection agency. In this respect, an effective resource community can be characterized as one in which the means for detecting free-riding behavior are distributed throughout the community.

With regard to the means of correcting free-riding behavior via modifications in individuals' economic payoffs, we should, I think, be concerned less with the specific mechanisms of enforcement—taxation, fines, confiscation of property, imprisonment, and so on—and more concerned with the overall character of the *source* of those mechanisms. One characteristic of the state is that within it there is typically a high degree of political specialization and division of political labor such that the power to affect the payoffs of individuals' behavior is concentrated in the hands of a relatively small number of individuals. In a community, such powers are typically more disbursed among its members. As Taylor writes, "to the extent that a society lacks political specialization and to the extent that force is dispersed, to that extent also must there be *equal participation* in whatever political functions remain."[30] In a community, the relative equality of powers to modify individuals' behavior is intimately connected to the relative equality of its members' participation in determining and wielding that power. In a resource community, the rationale for changing recalcitrant individuals' behavior is to get them to comply with an agreement about prudent resource use. One such individual may be more influenced by the threat of fines than by the threat of confiscation; another more by the threat of imprisonment; and so on. Moreover, confiscation, for example, may work better than a fine for improving the resource, or it may be the other way around. Such considerations indicate that the effectiveness of a communal approach to public goods provision will rely in many cases on the community members' overall ability to understand both the nature of resource and each other's expected reaction to different kinds of threats. That is, the greater the number of and degree to which members of a resource community participate in the process whereby free-riding behavior is combated through coercive mechanisms, the more effective that community will be in actually changing that behavior.

In summary, although we lack a rigorous conceptual analysis of "community," we still are able to say, albeit in rather general and relative terms, what distinguishes strong communities from weak ones. When a group of individuals share common beliefs and values about some important, common purpose, and when their relationship to one another vis-à-vis that purpose is direct and multifaceted, then they have at their disposal the means for becoming an *effective* community. When the purpose for which those individuals are so united is the improvement of a jointly used resource plagued by nonreciprocal externalities, then those individuals constitute a potentially effective *resource* community. There is a moral sensibility about right and wrong action at work in such communities, a sensibility that makes possible the employment of certain social mechanisms for combating free riding. There is little doubt that those social mechanisms will be insufficient for eliminating all free-riding behavior. But where both the means of detecting and the power of controlling such behavior can be relatively distributed throughout the community, free riding can be controlled effectively with a reduced reliance on coercive enforcement mechanisms.

TOWARD AN EFFECTIVE RESOURCE COMMUNITY IN THE WEST

A common-property arrangement is a form of resource management in which a group of co-owners collectively decides how its individual members should use a particular resource according to rules it establishes, promulgates, and enforces. If such an arrangement can be established and maintained for water in the Colorado River basin, and if that arrangement is successful in improving the resource, then it would constitute a viable approach to providing public goods with similar factor endowments. The river basin contains a multitude of users, spread out over thousands of square miles, whose various uses differently impact both the resource and each other. In such a state of affairs, an individual's expectations about others' self-restraint will be less than certain, and others' contributions often will be of a different character and scope than that individual's. Individuals' preference for coordinated activity, understood as a preference for doing the right thing when enough others can be expected to do the right thing too, will have to manifest itself as a widespread commitment to generalized reciprocity. Only in relatively strong communities can such commitments arise, flourish, and render effective the social mechanisms that reduce the need for coercive enforcement. So, the viability of a common-property arrangement for water in the West relies on creating the conditions necessary for a strong, effective community.

Water use in the Colorado River basin involves a large, loosely knit, and far-flung collection of individuals. Insofar as they recognize themselves as engaged in a common enterprise, they do so as inhabitants of particular places—Los Angeles, Phoenix, the Imperial Valley, the Grand Valley—or as members of particular user groups—irrigators, urban dwellers, industrialists, recreational users. Both individually and vis-à-vis their respective groups, they compete with one another for ever-increasing amounts of an increasingly scarce resource. The interaction between these groups is relatively infrequent, highly contentious, and often insincere; they tend to "communicate" with one another only in courtrooms, committee hearings, editorial columns, and the like. The overall tenor and character of this relationship is colored by each group's perception that others' beliefs and values about the resource are divergent if not wholly dissimilar from its own. This attitude serves to stifle discussion and the search for a common ground upon which to base a cooperative agreement. Clearly, that collection of individuals who eventually would make up an effective resource community in the West currently resembles a community in only a very weak sense of the term. In the remainder of this section, I tentatively suggest ways in which westerners can move toward becoming an effective resource community.

The first step in building a strong and potentially effective resource community is to disabuse individual users of the belief that either *nothing* at all needs to be done or that nothing needs to be done *by them*. As was discussed in chapters 1 and 2, the best available information clearly indicates that the current pattern of water use in the Colorado River basin cannot continue unabated. The belief that *something* has to be done, that there have to be some changes in overall use patterns, will only become more widespread if this information is promulgated to and internalized by all the basin's inhabitants. Along with information about the condition of the resource, we have good information about how individuals' various uses affect both the resource and each other. We can show irrigators, urban dwellers, and others how their particular uses affect the quantity and quality of water, and how changes in their activities will improve the resource. Until rather recently we had only quite vague notions about the interconnections among various uses, but we now understand in ever-increasing detail how specific changes will have predictable effects on the resource. By promulgating *this* information, individuals will come to understand how each of them can contribute to the improvement of the resource. Through gathering and promulgating information about the current state of the resource, about how individuals' uses affect both the resource and other users, and about how changes in each user's pattern of use can improve the resource, the perceptual gap that currently separates individuals and groups of water users will be greatly reduced.

This information can be promulgated through a variety of mediums and on many different scales. On a large scale, there are television, radio, periodicals, and, of ever-growing importance, the Internet. Shows, articles, advertisements, interviews, web pages, and the like are all effective means for influencing individuals' beliefs. On a somewhat smaller scale, the region's schools and universities could require their students to take courses on various aspects of water use in the West: a history course and/or a hydrology course. (Not unimportantly, this would most likely lead to more and better research in those areas, with obvious benefits.) And on a smaller scale still, booths could be set up at fairs and sporting events, talks could be held at bookstores and coffee houses, and so on. All things considered, westerners already have at their disposal broad and effective means for informing one another about the state of the resource and about ways of improving it. Taken together, these means enable more direct and multifaceted relationships to develop among the basin's inhabitants. In such an environment, individuals' beliefs can be aired, compared, tested, and reformulated such that each can see not only *that* but also *how* their lives are interconnected through the river they all share.

Once each water user believes that the resource is in jeopardy and that there is something particular and concrete that he or she can do to improve it, then his or her preference for coordinated activity may motivate more frequent, broad-based, and sincere discussions about how to improve the resource. In these discussions, the basin's inhabitants collectively would determine overall goals for resource, for example, target levels of flow rates, salt content, and so on, and specific ways of reaching those goals. These deliberations will most certainly be a reflexive, iterative, and ongoing process: various ends and means will be proposed, clarified, weighed against each other, changed, proposed again, and so on; as the state of the resource changes, so will the tenor of the deliberations. What ultimately would emerge, though, would be an acceptable set of rules about prudent water use. What is considered "prudent water use" for an urban dweller will be quite different than that for an irrigator, a recreational user, or an industrial user; that is, the content of these rules will be different for different groups of users. But the overall character of the particular rules would be the same: they would specify what sorts of self-restraining behavior constituted doing the right thing for each or each kind of water user. An urban dweller would know what is expected of him, an irrigator what is expected of her, and so on, and most crucially, each water user would know what is expected of the others. If a critical mass of water users can generate in one another mutual expectations of appropriate self-restraining behavior, then individuals' capacities to practice conditional cooperation can be activated and maintained, thereby making it more likely that free riding will not dominate cooperating.

Developing these rules will not be without its difficulties. But assuming that an acceptable set of rules does eventually emerge from such deliberations, we need to be concerned with how difficult it will be to actually monitor and enforce them so that free riding can be combated effectively. In order for those in the Colorado River basin to first establish and then maintain a common-property arrangement, rule breaking must be made easy to detect. Unless users' activities are relatively open, detecting free-riding behavior will be difficult and costly, and the community's ability to correct it, through either persuasive or coercive mechanisms, will be greatly reduced. Moreover, the more difficult it is for individuals to be assured that enough others are following the rules, the less likely it will be that they will choose to follow the rules themselves: individuals' capacity for generalized reciprocity cannot become operative when expectations of others' behavior are difficult to generate and verify. So, the viability of a common-property arrangement for water in the West depends on individual users' activities being relatively open for all to see. In the case of the Colorado River basin, such openness either already exists or can be established quite easily.

Most uses of water in the basin and *all* uses originally recognized under the doctrine of prior appropriation require diverting water out of the river, either to irrigate fields, to drive turbines, or to satisfy the various needs of urban dwellers. Both the diversions and uses occur at particular locations along the river or within the basin. At most of these locations, which include diversion gates, farms, factories, and urban homes, water meters are already installed and monitored such that detailed information about individuals' water use is readily available. Where these devices are not already in place they can be installed quite easily. At particular points along the river, especially just above and below where either significant return flows reenter the river system or where significant *in-stream* uses occur, we can install other devices, ones that measure the levels of salt and other contaminants in the river. Again, many of these measuring devices are already in place, and we can only get better and more detailed information by increasing both their accuracy and their number.

Simply gathering this information is not enough though; the information must also be readily available to everyone in the resource community. To take an extreme example, the willingness of a particular resident of Los Angeles to do his part to improve the resource relies to some extent on his assurance that an irrigator in Colorado is doing hers, and vice versa. The easier it is for both of them to see that the other is actually cooperating, the more likely it is that both will choose to do the right thing him- or herself. Direct observation by each of the other's activities is far from practical: the time and effort involved makes it prohibitive. However, by making information about both the irrigator's and urban dweller's water use available to everyone in the resource community, direct observation is not required for generating the requisite level of assurance. Local institutions, for example, rural and urban water companies, could be required to publish information obtained from individual monitoring devices. Alternatively, or in addition to such efforts, these various devices could be outfitted with transmitters, so that the information is sent directly to central computer locations and is then published in newspapers or made available on web sites. In order for an urban resident or irrigator to be assured that other water users, either close by or quite far away, are doing their part, he or she would then need to devote only a small amount of time and effort. In short, it is well within existing or readily available means to gather and promulgate to individuals reliable information about others' water usage, allowing each of them to determine with relative ease if others are in fact adhering to rules about prudent water use.

When what constitutes doing the right thing is clear to everyone in the basin, and when everyone's behavior is open for others to see, the various social mechanisms that reduce the need for coercive enforcement can work to curtail free-riding behavior quite effectively. The negative opinion of a resident of far-off Los Angeles may not cause a rule-breaking irrigator in the Grand Valley to feel any strong compunction to change her cheating ways. But if she continues to break the rules, then that activity can be easily detected by her neighbors, friends, and other close associates, who may then engage in various forms of social ostracism. If a wrongdoer finds that his or her ability to build and maintain relationships with those around him or her is negatively impacted by failing to comply with water use rules, then he or she may be persuaded to comply without the use of fines or other coercive mechanisms. Even inhabitants of the river basin who are quite far away may be able to exert palpable and persuasive pressure on free riders. For example, if the residents of Los Angeles discover, as they easily might, that one or several fruit growers in the Imperial Valley are not complying with prudent water use rules, then those residents might express their displeasure by boycotting Imperial Valley fruit. Or, if Los Angeles as a whole fails to cooperate, then upstream users might simply return to their wasteful ways. The general point here is that, as the ability of others to detect free riding increases, so will increase the variety and effectiveness of social mechanisms for motivating compliance. As compliance becomes more widespread, individuals' expectations of others' cooperative behavior will increase, thereby making it more likely that individuals' preference for coordinated activity can be activated and maintained at a level where free riding is less attractive.

There will of course be those individuals who will still attempt to cheat. For them, only the palpable threat of coercive measures will serve to modify their behavior. The effectiveness of such measures is intimately connected to the ease with which such behavior can be detected: before cheating can be corrected it first needs to be discovered. Because an individual's water use can be easily monitored, most attempts to cheat will be open to detection. Discovery of cheating becomes more likely when there is widespread and active participation among the basin's inhabitants in monitoring each other's activities. We should expect such participation at the inception of a common-property arrangement because the activation of individuals' preference for coordinated activity relies on their assurance that enough others are in fact doing the right thing. And if some free-riding behavior is discovered and is expected to continue to occur as time goes on, we can also expect a continuing effort by others to monitor individuals' activities. Within the river basin cheating *can* be discovered quite easily; and ongoing cheating will only serve to perpetuate and intensify efforts to monitor individuals' activities, so that such behavior likely *will* be discovered. One requirement for an effective resource community is the ease with which free riding can be uncovered without the need for creating a centralized detection agency; such is indeed the case in the Colorado River basin.

If left uncorrected, even rather limited instances of free-riding behavior may serve to erode others' propensity to continue cooperating. Therefore, the basin's inhabitants are confronted with the task of forcing recalcitrant individuals to comply with water use rules through developing and implementing coercive enforcement mechanisms. The nature of the resource suggests that a single, centralized source for this task will be less effective than various, localized sources. The more distant an agency is from a given issue, the less well informed it will tend to be about that issue, and hence the less effective it will likely be in dealing with that issue.[31] For the Colorado River basin, the resource's size, the number of users, the variety of uses to which it is put, and the variability of external effects caused by those uses all point to the need to create a variety of institutions tailored to particular uses, users, and locations. Urban dwellers are likely to have a better grasp of their needs, problems, and so on than are irrigators, recreational users, or industrial users; individuals in Los Angeles or irrigators in the Imperial Valley will have their own issues, ones not wholly shared by the residents of Phoenix or farmers in the Grand Valley; and residents of a certain neighborhood within a city or growers of a certain crop within a farming region will have more particular issues still. Such considerations indicate that the creation of various localized institutions for combating free riding will enhance the prospects of eliminating such behavior: neighborhood associations, farming cooperatives, recreational user groups, and so on.

In order to be effective, such institutions will require the widespread and active participation of users in particular locations and engaged in particular activities. This is the final characteristic of an effective resource community: The greater the number of and degree to which members of a resource community participate in the process whereby free-riding behavior is combated through coercive mechanisms, the more effective that community will be in actually changing that behavior.

Changes in water use rules, engendered by changes in the ways the basin's inhabitants view the resource and interact with one another, will most certainly result in changes in the character and scope of existing institutions. At one end of the spectrum, there are large-scale state and federal institutions (legislatures, courts, agencies, and so on); at the other end, there are small-scale, local institutions (neighborhood associations, farming cooperatives, recreational user groups, and the like). Presently, the former sorts of institutions mainly conduct the establishment and enforcement of water use rules. Certain aspects of establishing a common-property arrangement in the basin—installing monitoring devices, outfitting them with transmission capabilities, creating databases, and so on—may require the resources available to large-scale state and federal institutions. And maintaining such an arrangement will no doubt require some measure of coordinated, large-scale oversight, so that we should not expect such institutions to disappear altogether.[32] In the long run, however, institutions of the latter sort will be more and more relied upon to maintain the arrangement.

The effectiveness of small-scale, local, and personalized social institutions for providing a public good relies on there being widespread and active participation by the resource users, that is, on their coming together and operating as members of an effective resource community. As I will discuss, the same general features of such a community constitute the core elements of *civic republican* notions about political obligation. The civic republican tradition rests squarely on a face-to-face, hands-on approach to problem solving, with its implicit belief that people can rise above their particular interests to pursue a common goal.[33] Contemporary advocates of civic republicanism have been noticeably silent, vague, or both about the overall character of property-rights arrangements that would be consistent with their preferred notion of political obligation.[34] The conditions necessary for creating a common-property arrangement are the same as those required for creating civic republican political institutions; therefore, such an arrangement can be viewed as a concrete expression of a republican notion of political obligation. In other words, by creating a common-property arrangement for water, westerners would in effect be creating a water republic.

CONCLUSION: TOWARD A WATER REPUBLIC

The American West was settled by a group of individuals who wholeheartedly embraced the idea that rugged individualism was the quality that would best preserve them. They adopted a political and economic framework that takes as its ideal the autonomy of individual agents. By permitting each individual to pursue vigorously his or her own private interests, the settlers believed that the general good would emerge without anyone having bothered to will it deliberately into existence. However, individuals' pursuit of their own private satisfactions has resulted in the depletion and degradation of the West's most vital resource—water—to the detriment of everyone concerned. The nature of the resource is such that only a conscious and deliberate effort by the region's inhabitants will suffice to secure their individual and collective well being. As Wallace Stegner wrote over thirty years ago, "When [the West] fully learns that cooperation, not rugged individualism, is the quality that most characterizes and preserves it, then it will have achieved itself and outlived its origins."[35] Such cooperation will require a shift in the cultural and institutional setting within which the region's inhabitants currently interact with one another. Rather than continuing to depend on the invisible hand of the marketplace, westerners should embrace small-scale units of government, where individuals can engage one another directly, intensively, and repeatedly enough to come to know, desire, and pursue their common good together. This state of affairs constitutes the basis of a civic republican, or simply republican, notion of political obligation.

Within the republican tradition, the merely "economic man" is considered less than fully human: "Assuming a certain tension between public good and private desires, [republicans] will identify the unrestrained pursuit of purely private interests as incompatible with the preservation of a commonwealth."[36] The ideal republican agent is a *citizen*, someone who is disposed to "further public over private good in action and deliberation."[37] Citizens' sense of collective responsibility manifests itself in their active and informed participation in public affairs; this constitutes an individual's citizenship. In other words, republican citizens have a preference for coordinated activity as such, and their willingness to practice cooperation, that is, their willingness to practice citizenship, is an instantiation of generalized reciprocal behavior.

The moral sensibility that forms the basis for effective republican citizenship is labeled "civility," which, in general, "is a matter of internalizing values that stretch people's desires beyond the compass of narrow, selfish concerns."[38] The most important of those values, or *civic virtues*, is trust, which, to be internalized, requires that citizens be fair and honest in their dealings with one another: "Nothing will substitute for those virtues; nothing else will get the job done."[39] Recognizing that civility can only develop over time and among a group of intimately connected individuals, republicans advocate small-scale units of government, where individuals can be engaged with one another directly, intensively, and repeatedly enough to come to know and desire the common good.[40] In short, citizens of a republic display the attributes of individuals playing an Assurance Game, rather than individuals caught up in either a one-shot or iterated Prisoner's Dilemma.

In order to manifest itself, citizenship requires some focus, some object or goal, that cannot be achieved without a cooperative effort. Contemporary advocates of republicanism maintain that the preferences and practices indicative of citizenship are most likely to arise when public or common goods are involved. Their description of such goods mirrors economists': "A good will be common to the extent that it cannot be increased (or decreased) for any member of the relevant group without at the same time being increased (or decreased) for other members of the group: it has the sort of non-excludability economists ascribe to goods like clean air."[41] Individuals who recognize that their activities both affect and are affected by others may be sufficiently motivated to try to work together toward improving that good. Water in the West appears to be just the sort of resource for which republican notions about political obligation are intended.

Once a common goal is identified, an individual's willingness to contribute to that goal can be activated and maintained only when he or she expects enough others to do likewise. Citizens of a republic have to trust one another, and trust arises only through observing the behavior of others over time. That is, only when individuals have direct and multifaceted interactions with one another can the requisite level of trust be generated. As I argued earlier, the relative openness of individuals' water use in the West is such that generating that level of trust, and hence enabling individuals to practice republican citizenship, can be achieved quite easily.

There has been a renewed interest of late in articulating the core features of republicanism and in exploring how that tradition relates to both classical and contemporary ideas about liberalism. Some theorists have argued that the two traditions are really complementary aspects of a single notion about political obligation; others maintain that they are separable but mutually supportive traditions; and still others insist that embracing one of the traditions entails a rejection of the other.[42] Such matters are well beyond the scope of the discussion here. However, what is important to recognize is that republicanism represents a recognizable form of political obligation with a rich tradition within political philosophy. And a common-property arrangement constitutes a concrete instantiation of that tradition. Therefore, those who, like Ophuls, believe that the sort of ecological scarcity facing westerners today requires new and unpalatable forms of political institutions are being unduly, and unnecessarily, apocalyptic.

Insofar as a common-property arrangement represents a republican vision of political obligation, there is one aspect of such arrangements that might be seen as an impediment to the creation and maintenance of such an arrangement for water in the West. Advocates of republicanism have in the past supposed that self-governing associations that rely on the effective operation of civic virtues are only possible across relatively small geographic regions. Republics must be small, they argued, so that individuals can be engaged with one another intensively and repeatedly enough to come to know and desire the common good.[43] However, the forms of information, modes of transportation, and means of communication available in the early twenty-first century serve to expand the physical limitations of potential republics: People's expanded ability to interact with one another, influence each others' beliefs, and generate mutual expectations sufficient for generalized reciprocal behavior to manifest itself are no longer bound by seventeenth-century notions of community.

There is another aspect of republicanism that is worrisome to some: the potentially stifling effect that community-based, or communitarian, forms of authority may have on nonconformists. Such worries are not unfounded; historically, communities organized around moral convictions have often treated quite harshly those living within them who deviated from the reigning orthodoxy. Hence, for some proponents of liberalism, if compulsion is necessary for forcing free riders into compliance, then "macro-constraints are vastly preferred to micro-constraints. That is, limitations on our freedom that are indirect, remote, and impersonal are preferred to those that are direct, proximate, and personal."[44] Such worries cannot be extinguished altogether. But a common-property arrangement for water in the West takes as its starting point a material fact, the depleted and degraded state of the resource, and as long as *that* remains the basis upon which the region's inhabitants limit one another's activities, then the community may be able to mitigate against possible abuses of its power. By being as inclusive as possible, by continually reevaluating the state of the resource, and by readjusting use rules as conditions change, the community of resource users need not succumb to the tyranny of the majority. Understanding the various pitfalls strewn across their path, westerners have a good chance of avoiding them.

The imperatives of a place should play a role in shaping its overall social order: A people's culture and institutions must be responsive to the circumstances in which they find themselves, and different circumstances may well require different cultural and institutional arrangements. This is nowhere more evident than in the Colorado River basin. The imperatives of the region, the fact that the lives of those who live in the basin are physically connected through the one river that they all share, are such that neither urban dwellers, nor farmers, nor anyone else can thrive in the way they would prefer unless and until they focus their attention more directly on one another and come to embrace the idea that they are, in the words of Daniel Kemmis, "mutually complementary parts of the enterprise of inhabiting this place."[45] This refocusing constitutes a shift away from narrowly self-interested thinking and behavior, toward a more interdependent and public mode of existence. Such a way of life conjures up a political and social philosophy that can be traced back to Aristotle, who envisioned people as citizens of a commonwealth in which they both ruled and were ruled in turn by one another.[46] A

common-property arrangement, where each resource user partici-
pates in the process whereby the rules of his or her use are collectively determined, constitutes such a commonwealth. By reappropriat-
ing this republican tradition, we have a political philosophy to which
such a shift can be directed. Insofar as republican ideas have faded
from our midst, retrieving them constitutes recovering a lost vision
of what public life might be like. Reanimating republican institutions is neither atavistic nor nostalgic; rather, I see it as a for-
ward-looking vision of what the West might, and *should*, aspire to.

Rather than being pessimistic about the West, we should be hope-
ful about it; indeed, the American West has been called the native
home of hope. By creating a common-property arrangement for its
most precious of resources, the West has a chance, perhaps its last, to,
as Stegner puts it, "create a society to match its scenery."[47] Such is
the belief that has motivated this book.

NOTES

1. William Ophuls, "Leviathan or Oblivion," in *Toward a Steady State Economy*, ed. Herman Daly (San Francisco: Freeman, 1973), 228; see also Russell Hardin, *Collective Action* (Baltimore, MD: Johns Hopkins University for Resources for the Future, 1982), 25.

2. Gregory Marwell and Ronald Ames, "Economists Free Ride, Does Anyone Else?: Experiments in the Provision of Public Goods IV," *Journal of Public Economics* 15 (1981): 297.

3. See Amartya K. Sen, "Isolation, Assurance and the Social Rate of Discount," *Quarterly Journal of Economics* 81 (1967): 114; and Amartya K. Sen, *On Economic Inequality*, 2d ed. (Oxford: Clarendon, 1997), 98–99.

4. This is not to say that self-interest is unimportant, or that people are mostly concerned with *other* people's welfare. I agree with Jane J. Mansbridge that "self interest explains most of human interaction in some contexts, and it plays some role in almost every context." See Jane J. Mansbridge, Preface to *Beyond Self-Interest*, ed. Jane J. Mansbridge (Chicago: University of Chicago Press, 1990), ix. All I, and I think anyone else, is saying is that there is more to human motivation than narrow self-interest.

5. Elinor Ostrom and James Walker, "Communication in a Commons: Cooperation without External Enforcement," in *Laboratory Research in Political Economy*, ed. Thomas Palfrey (Ann Arbor: University of Michigan Press, 1991), 317; see also Elinor Ostrom, James Walker, and Roy Gardner, "Covenants with and without a Sword: Self-Governance Is Possible," *American Political Science Review* 82, no. 2 (June 1992): 404–417.

6. Donald Worster, *Rivers of Empire: Water, Aridity, and the Growth of the American West* (New York: Random House, Pantheon Books, 1985; reprint, New York: Oxford University Press, 1992), 280; see also Daniel

Kemmis, *Community and the Politics of Place* (Norman: University of Oklahoma Press, 1990), 11–16.

7. William Ophuls, *Ecology and the Politics of Scarcity Revisited* (New York: Freeman, 1992), 200, 217.

8. See C. Ford Runge, "Institutions and the Free Rider: The Assurance Problem in Collective Action," *Journal of Politics* 46 (1984): 158.

9. Glenn G. Stevenson, *Common Property Economics: A General Theory and Land Use Applications* (Cambridge: Cambridge University Press, 1991), 74.

10. See Runge, "Institutions and the Free Rider," 158

11. Martin Shubik, "Game Theory, Behavior and the Paradox of the Prisoner's Dilemma: Three Solutions," *Journal of Conflict Resolution* 14 (1970): 190; see also Michael Taylor, *The Possibility of Cooperation* (Cambridge: Cambridge University Press, 1987), xi, 18–19.

12. Stevenson, *Common Property Economics*, 75.

13. Sen, "Isolation, Assurance and the Social Rate of Discount," 114.

14. Jon Elster, *Ulysses and the Sirens: Studies in Rationality and Irrationality* (Cambridge: Cambridge University Press, 1984), 21.

15. In fact, Sen has recently changed his position that individuals will prefer to cooperate only in the special case of universal compliance. See Amartya K. Sen, "Rational Fools: A Critique of the Behavioral Foundations of Economic Theory," in *Beyond Self-Interest*, ed. Jane H. Mansbridge (Chicago: University of Chicago Press, 1990), 40–41.

16. See Jane J. Mansbridge, "The Rise and Fall of Self-Interest in the Explanation of Political Life," in *Beyond Self-Interest*, ed. Jane H. Mansbridge (Chicago: University of Chicago Press, 1990), 17; and Runge, "Institutions and the Free Rider," 158–161.

17. Runge "Institutions and the Free Rider," 161.

18. Michael Taylor, *Community, Anarchy and Liberty* (Cambridge: Cambridge University Press, 1982), 29.

19. Runge, "Institutions and the Free Rider," 162.

20. See Sen, *On Economic Inequality*, 98

21. John Rawls, *Political Liberalism* (New York: Columbia University Press, 1993), 49.

22. Ibid., 50.

23. For a different view, see Richard Dagger, *Civic Virtues* (New York: Oxford University Press, 1997), 108–110.

24. Sen, "Rational Fools," 31–33.

25. See Mansbridge, "Rise and Fall of Self-Interest," 19–20.

26. Alan Gewirth, *The Community of Rights* (Chicago: University of Chicago Press, 1996), 88.

27. Taylor, *Community, Anarchy and Liberty*, 26.

28. In a virtual community, the members' interactions are such that *direct* interactions, as we ordinarily conceive of them, are absent altogether. In order to include such a state of affairs within the ambit of communities, direct interaction may have to be reconsidered; perhaps "unmediated by

institutions" is a better way to think about the interactions in such communities. See Taylor, *Community, Anarchy and Liberty*, 27–28.

29. See Taylor, *Community, Anarchy and Liberty*, 19–20, 83–88; and Ostrom and Walker, "Communication in a Commons," 303–305.

30. Taylor, *Community, Anarchy and Liberty*, 10, emphasis in original.

31. For similar remarks, see Philip Pettit, *Republicanism* (Oxford: Oxford University Press, 1997), 153.

32. The remote possibility exists that an entire city or farming region could act in bad faith, by cheating and then attempting to conceal its activities from others in the basin. Hence, some institution charged with general oversight, for example, a basin-wide detection agency, may be required.

33. See Kemmis, *Community and the Politics of Place*, 11.

34. See Dagger, *Civic Virtues*, 15; Gewirth, *Community of Rights*, chapter 5; and Pettit, *Republicanism*, 135.

35. Wallace Stegner, *The Sound of Mountain Water* (New York: Doubleday, 1969), 38.

36. Lance Banning, "Jeffersonian Ideology Revisited: Liberal and Classical Ideas in the New American Republic," *William and Mary Quarterly* 43 (January 1986): 11–12.

37. Dagger, *Civic Virtues*, 14; see also Shelley Burtt, "The Good Citizen's Psyche: On the Psychology of Civic Virtue," *Polity* 23 (Fall 1990): 24.

38. Pettit, *Republicanism*, 257.

39. Kemmis, *Community and the Politics of Place*, 133.

40. Ibid., 11–13.

41. Pettit, *Republicanism*, 121; see also Dagger, *Civic Virtues*, 68–73; and Taylor, *Community, Anarchy and Liberty*, 39–44.

42. See Dagger, *Civic Virtues*, for the first position, Gewirth, *Community of Rights*, especially chapter 1, for the second, and Pettit, *Republicanism*, for the third.

43. See Charles-Louis Secondat, Baron de Montesquieu, *The Spirit of Laws*, bk. 7, trans. Thomas Nugent (London: George Bell, 1906), chapter 16, 130; and Kemmis, *Community and the Politics of Place*, 16–18.

44. Ophuls, *Ecology and the Politics of Scarcity Revisited*, 212–213; see also Pettit, *Republicanism*, 153.

45. Kemmis, *Community and the Politics of Place*, 124.

46. See Aristotle, "Politics," in *The Collected Works of Aristotle*, ed. Richard McKeon (New York: Random House, 1941), 1283b42–1284a2.

47. Stegner, *Sound of Mountain Water*, 39.

Selected Bibliography

Anderson, Terry L., ed. *Water Rights: Scarce Resource Allocation, Bureaucracy, and the Environment*. Cambridge, MA: Ballinger Publishing for the Pacific Institute for Public Policy Research, 1983.

Anderson, Terry L., and P. J. Hill, "The Evolution of Property Rights: A Study of the American West." *Journal of Law and Economics* 18 (1975): 163—179.

————. "From Free Grass to Fences: Transforming the Commons of the American West." In *Managing the Commons*, ed. Garrett Hardin and John Baden, 200–216. New York: Freeman, 1977.

Anderson, Terry L., and Donald R. Leal. *Free Market Environmentalism*. San Francisco: Westview Press for the Pacific Institute for Public Policy Research, 1991.

Aristotle. "Politics." In *The Collected Works of Aristotle*. Ed. Richard McKeon. New York: Random House, 1941.

Arnold, N. Scott. "Economists and Philosophers as Critics of the Free Enterprise System." *The Monist* 73, no. 4 (October 1990): 621–641.

Banning, Lance. "Jeffersonian Ideology Revisited: Liberal and Classical Ideas in the New American Republic." *William and Mary Quarterly* 43 (January 1986): 3–19.

Becker, Lawrence C. "The Moral Basis of Property Rights." In *Property*, ed. J. Roland Pennock and John W. Chapman, 187–220. New York: New York University Press, 1980.

————. *Property Rights: Philosophic Foundations*. London: Routledge and Kegan Paul, 1977.

————. "Too Much Property." *Philosophy and Public Affairs* 21 (1992): 196–206.

Berkes, Fikret. "Success and Failure in Marine Coastal Fisheries of Turkey." In *Making the Commons Work*, ed. Daniel W. Bromley et al., 161–182. San Francisco: Institute for Contemporary Studies, 1992.

Bierman, H. Scott, and Luis Fernandez. *Game Theory with Economic Applications*. Reading, MA: Addison-Wesley, 1993.

Blackstone, William. *Commentaries on the Laws of England*. 11th ed. Bk. 2. London: Strahan and Woodfall, 1791.

Boyan, A. Stephan, Jr. Forward to *Ecology and the Politics of Scarcity*, by William Ophuls. New York: Freeman, 1992.

Bromley, Daniel W. "The Commons, Property, and Common-Property Regimes." In *Making the Commons Work*, ed. Daniel W. Bromley et al., 3–16. San Francisco: Institute for Contemporary Studies, 1992.

————. *Environment and Economy: Property Rights and Public Policy*. Oxford: Basil Blackwell, 1991.

Burtt, Shelley. "The Good Citizen's Psyche: On the Psychology of Civic Virtue." *Polity* 23 (Fall 1990): 23–38.

Carrier, Jim. *The Colorado: A River at Risk*. Englewood, CO: Westcliffe, 1992.

Chapman, John W. "Justice, Freedom, and Property." In *Property*, ed. J. Roland Pennock and John W. Chapman, 289–324. New York: New York University Press, 1980.

Ciriacy-Wantrup, S. V. "Water Quality, a Problem for the Economist." *Journal of Farm Economics* 153 (1961): 1133–1144.

Ciriacy-Wantrup, S. V., and Richard C. Bishop. "'Common Property' as a Concept in Natural Resources Policy." *Natural Resources Journal* 15, no. 4 (October 1975): 713–727.

Coase, Ronald H. "The Problem of Social Cost." *Law and Economics* 3 (October 1960): 1–44.

Colorado River Compact of 1922. Pub. L. No. 56 (codified as amended at 43 U.S.C. § 617 et seq.).

Cuzán, Alfred Z. "Appropriators versus Expropriators: The Political Economy of Water in the West." In *Water Rights: Scarce Resource Allocation, Bureaucracy, and the Environment*, ed. Terry L. Anderson, 13–41. Cambridge, MA: Ballinger Publishing for the Pacific Institute for Public Policy Research, 1983.

Dagger, Richard. *Civic Virtues*. New York: Oxford University Press, 1997.

Day, J. P. "Locke on Property." *Philosophical Quarterly* 16 (July 1966): 207–220.

Demsetz, Harold. "Toward a Theory of Property Rights." *American Economic Review, Papers and Proceedings* 57 (1967): 347–359.

Dworkin, Ronald. "What Is Equality? Part 2: Equality of Resources." *Philosophy and Public Affairs* 10, no. 4 (Fall 1981): 283–345.

Ellickson, Robert C. *Order without Law*. Cambridge, MA: Harvard University Press, 1991.

Elster, Jon. *Ulysses and the Sirens: Studies in Rationality and Irrationality*. Cambridge: Cambridge University Press, 1984.

Epstein, Richard A.. "On the Optimal Mix of Private and Common Property." In *Property Rights*, ed. Ellen Frankel Paul, Fred D. Miller Jr., and Jeffery Paul, 17–41. Cambridge: Cambridge University Press, 1994.

Fradkin, Philip L. *A River No More: The Colorado River and the West*. Tucson: University of Arizona Press, 1981.

Gewirth, Alan. *The Community of Rights*. Chicago: University of Chicago Press, 1996.

Goldfarb, William. *Water Law*. 2d ed. Chelsea, MI: Lewis, 1988.

Gopalakrishnan, Chennat. "The Doctrine of Prior Appropriation and Its Impact on Water Development." *The American Journal of Economics and Sociology* 32 (1973): 61–72.

Grey, Thomas C. "The Disintegration of Property." In *Property*, ed. J. Roland Pennock and John W. Chapman, 69–85. New York: New York University Press, 1980.

Grunebaum, James O. *Private Ownership*. London: Routledge and Kegan Paul, 1987.

Hardin, Garrett. "The Tragedy of the Commons." *Science* 162 (1968): 1243–1248. Reprinted in *Managing the Commons*, ed. Garrett Hardin and John Baden, 16–30. New York: Freeman, 1977.

Hardin, Russell. *Collective Action*. Baltimore, MD: Johns Hopkins University for Resources for the Future, 1982.

Hart, H.L.A. *The Concept of Law*. Oxford: Oxford University Press, 1961.

Hawkins, Robert B. Forward to *Making the Commons Work*, ed. Daniel W. Bromley et al., xi–xii. San Francisco: Institute for Contemporary Studies, 1992.

Held, Virginia. *Property, Profits, and Economic Justice*. Belmont, WA: Wadsworth, 1980.

Hirshleifer, Jack, James DeHaven, and Jerome Milliman. *Water Supply*. Chicago: University of Chicago Press, 1969.

Hohfeld, Wesley Newcomb. *Fundamental Legal Conceptions as Applied in Judicial Reasoning*. Ed. Walter W. Cook. New Haven, CT: Yale University Press, 1919.

Honoré, A. M. "Ownership." In *Making Law Bind*. Oxford: Clarendon, 1987.

Horwitz, Morton. *The Transformation of American Law, 1780–1860*. Cambridge, MA: Harvard University Press, 1977.

Hume, David. *Enquiries concerning Human Understanding and concerning the Principles of Morals*. 3d ed. Ed. L. A. Selby-Bigge. Nidditch. Oxford: Clarendon, 1975.

———. *A Treatise of Human Nature*. Ed. L. A. Selby-Bigge. Oxford: Clarendon, 1888.

Hundley, Norris, Jr. *Water and the West: The Colorado River Compact and the Politics of Water in the American West.* Berkeley: University of California Press, 1975.

Kemmis, Daniel. *Community and the Politics of Place.* Norman: University of Oklahoma Press, 1990.

Kymlicka, Will. *Contemporary Political Thought: An Introduction.* Oxford: Oxford University Press, 1990.

Locke, John. *Two Treatises of Government.* 2 vols. Ed. Peter Laslett. Cambridge: Cambridge University Press, 1988.

Maloney, Frank E. *A Model Water Code: With Commentary.* Gainesville: University of Florida Press, 1972.

Mansbridge, Jane J., ed. *Beyond Self-Interest.* Chicago: University of Chicago Press, 1990.

Marwell, Gregory, and Ronald Ames. "Economists Free Ride, Does Anyone Else?: Experiments in the Provision of Public Goods IV." *Journal of Public Economics* 15 (1981): 295–310.

Mautner, Thomas. "Locke on Original Appropriation." *American Philosophical Quarterly* 19, no. 3 (July 1982): 259–269.

McCool, Daniel C., ed. *Command of the Waters: Iron Triangles, Federal Water Development, and Indian Water.* Tucson: University of Arizona Press, 1994.

———. *Waters of Zion: The Politics of Water in Utah.* Salt Lake City: University of Utah Press, 1995.

McRuer, John D. "Conventions vs. Greens." *World* 63 (March–April 1990): 5–6.

Montesquieu, Charles-Louis Secondat, Baron de. *The Spirit of Laws.* Bk. 7. Trans. Thomas Nugent. London: George Bell, 1906.

Munzer, Stephen P. *A Theory of Property.* Cambridge: Cambridge University Press, 1990.

Narveson, Jan. "The Concept of Resources and Claims about Global Scarcities." Paper presented at the annual meeting of the Canadian Philosophical Association, Memorial University, St. John's, Newfoundland, June 1, 1997. In the possession of the author.

———. "Resources and Environmental Policy." *Philosophic Exchange* 23/24 (1993–1994): 39–61.

Newlands Act of 1902. Pub. L. No. 104–98, 32 Stat. 388 (codified as amended in scattered sections of 43 U.S.C.).

North, Douglas, and Robert P. Thomas. "The First Economic Revolution." *Economic History Review* 30 (1977): 229–241.

Nozick, Robert. *Anarchy, State, and Utopia.* New York: Basic, 1974.

Oakerson, Ronald J. "Analyzing the Commons: A Framework." In *Making the Commons Work,* ed. Daniel W. Bromley et at., 41–59. San Francisco: Institute for Contemporary Studies, 1992.

Ophuls, William. *Ecology and the Politics of Scarcity Revisited.* New York: Freeman, 1992.

————. "Leviathan or Oblivion." In *Toward a Steady State Economy*, ed. Herman Daly, 215–230. San Francisco: Freeman, 1973.

Ostrom, Elinor, and James Walker. "Communication in a Commons: Cooperation without External Enforcement." In *Laboratory Research in Political Economy*, ed. Thomas Palfrey, 287–321. Ann Arbor: University of Michigan Press, 1991.

Ostrom, Elinor, James Walker, and Roy Gardner. "Covenants with and without a Sword: Self-Governance Is Possible." *American Political Science Review* 82, no. 2 (June 1992): 404–417.

Pettit, Philip. "Free Riding and Foul Dealing." *The Journal of Philosophy* 83, no. 7 (July 1986): 361–379.

————. *Republicanism*. Oxford: Oxford University Press, 1997.

Pisani, Donald J. *Water, Land, and Law in the West*. Lawrence: University of Kansas Press, 1996.

Postel, Sandra. "Water Scarcity." *Environmental Science and Technology* 26 (1992): 2332–2333.

Powell, John Wesley. *Report on the Lands of the Arid Regions of the United States*. Cambridge, MA: Harvard University Press, 1962.

Raiklin, Ernest, and Bulent Uyarm. "On the Relativity of the Concept of Needs, Wants, Scarcity, and Opportunity Costs." *International Journal of Social Economics* 23, no. 7 (July 1996): 49–57.

Rashdall, Hastings. "The Philosophical Theory of Property." In *Property: Its Duties and Rights*. London: Macmillan, 1913.

Rawls, John. *Political Liberalism*. New York: Columbia University Press, 1993.

Reisner, Mark. *Cadillac Desert: The American West and Its Disappearing Water*. New York: Penguin, 1993.

Rose, Carol M. *Property and Persuasion*. Boulder, CO: Westview, 1994.

Runge, C. Ford. "Common Property and Collective Action in Economic Development." In *Making the Commons Work*, ed. Daniel W. Bromley et al., 17–40. San Francisco: Institute for Contemporary Studies, 1992.

————. "Institutions and the Free Rider: The Assurance Problem in Collective Action." *The Journal of Politics* 46 (1984): 154–181.

Ryan, Alan. "Self-Ownership, Autonomy, and Property Rights." In *Property*, ed. J. Roland Pennock and John W. Chapman, 221–247. New York: New York University Press, 1980.

Sahlins, Marshall. *Stone Age Economics*. New York: Aldine, 1972.

Sandel, Michael. *Democracy's Discontent*. Cambridge, MA: Harvard University Press, 1996.

Sassower, Ralph. "Scarcity and Setting the Boundaries of Political Economy." *Social Epistemology* 4 (1990): 75–91.

Sen, Amartya K. "Isolation, Assurance and the Social Rate of Discount." *Quarterly Journal of Economics* 81 (1967): 112–124.

————. *On Economic Inequality*. 2d ed. Oxford: Clarendon, 1997.

————. "Rational Fools: A Critique of the Behavioral Foundations of Economic Theory." In *Beyond Self-Interest*, ed. Jane J. Mansbridge, 25–43. Chicago: University of Chicago Press, 1990.

Shubik, Martin. "Game Theory, Behavior and the Paradox of the Prisoner's Dilemma: Three Solutions." *Journal of Conflict Resolution* 14 (1970): 181–193.

Simmons, A. John. "Historical Rights and Fair Shares." *Law and Philosophy* 14 (1995): 149–184.

————. *The Lockean Theory of Rights*. Princeton, NJ: Princeton University Press, 1992.

————. *On the Edge of Anarchy*. Princeton, NJ: Princeton University Press, 1993.

————. "Original-Acquisition Justifications of Private Property." *Social Philosophy and Policy* 11, no. 2 (Summer 1994): 63–84.

Stegner, Wallace. *Beyond the Hundredth Meridian: John Wesley Powell and the Second Opening of the West*. Lincoln: University of Nebraska Press, 1982.

————. "How the West Was Lost." In *A Sense of Place*. Niwot, CO: Audio, 1989.

————. *The Sound of Mountain Water*. New York: Doubleday, 1969.

Stevenson, Glenn G. *Common Property Economics: A General Theory and Land Use Applications*. Cambridge: Cambridge University Press, 1991.

Taylor, Michael. *Community, Anarchy and Liberty*. Cambridge: Cambridge University Press, 1982.

————. *The Possibility of Cooperation*. Cambridge: Cambridge University Press, 1987.

Tregarthen, Timothy D. "Water in Colorado: Fear and Loathing of the Marketplace." In *Water Rights*, ed. Terry L. Anderson, 119–135. Cambridge, MA: Ballinger Publishing for the Pacific Institute for Public Policy Research, 1983.

Trelease, Frank J. "The Model Water Code: The Wise Administrator and the Goddam Bureaucrat." *Natural Resources Journal* 14 (April 1974): 207–229.

————. "Uneasy Federalism-State Water Laws and National Water Uses." *Washington Law Review* 55 (November 1980): 752–753.

Varner, Gary. "Environmental Law and the Eclipse of Land as Private Property." In *Ethics and Environmental Policy*. Athens: University of Georgia Press, 1994.

Waldron, Jeremy. "The Advantages and Difficulties of the Humean Theory of Property." *Social Philosophy and Policy* 11, no. 2 (1994): 85–123.

————. *The Right to Private Property*. Oxford: Clarendon, 1988.

Webb, Walter Prescott. *The Great Plains*. Waltham, MA: Blaisdell, 1959.

Weber, Max. *Economy and Society*. Ed. Guenther Roth and Claus Wittich. Berkeley: University of California Press, 1968.

Worster, Donald. *Rivers of Empire: Water, Aridity, and the Growth of the American West*. New York: Random House, Pantheon Books, 1985; reprint, New York: Oxford University Press, 1992.

Xenos, Nicholas. "Liberalism and the Politics of Scarcity." *Political Theory* 15 (1987): 225–243.

———. *Scarcity and Modernity*. New York: Routledge, 1989.

Index

ABOUT THE AUTHOR

EDWARD M. BARBANELL is Assistant Dean for Undergraduate Studies, University of Utah. In addition, Professor Barbanell teaches philosophy and is the coeditor of *The Encyclopedia of Empiricism* (Greenwood Press, 1997).